WORKING WITH

Earth Energies

How to tap into the healing powers of the natural world

David Furlong

piatkus

PIATKUS

First published in Great Britain in 2003 by Judy Piatkus (Publishers) Limited
This edition published in Great Britain in 2017 by Piatkus

A CIP catalogue record for this book
is available from the British Library.

ISBN 978-0-7499-5855-8

Typeset by Action Publishing Technology Ltd
Printed and bound in Great Britain by CPI Group (UK) Ltd, Croydon, CRO 4YY

Edited by Ian Paten
Illustrations by Rodney Paull
Text design by Zena Flax

Papers used by Piatkus are from well-managed forests
and other responsible sources.

Piatkus
An imprint of
Little, Brown Book Group
50 Victoria Embankment
London EC4Y 0DZ

An Hachette UK Company
www.hachette.co.uk

To Gaia/Geb

About the Author

David Furlong holds a PhD degree in 'Transpersonal Counselling' with the University of Sedona, USA. He can be contacted through his website www.davidfurlong.co.uk

Copyright notice

Contents

Introduction

The destructive power of nature, through floods, hurricanes, earthquakes and volcanic activity has often dominated world news in recent years. Many people believe that the weather patterns have become more erratic, with warm days occurring in the middle of winters and biting cold days in normally warm summer months.

To an extent science backs up this intuitive perception, with global warming being cited as the main cause. However, scientists are also beginning to discover the complexity of the Earth's climate over the preceding millennia and have come to realise that fluctuations in the weather patterns of our world are driven by many complex factors, each of which can have enormous consequences.

Thirteen thousand years ago the Earth was in the grip of an ice age, which rendered much of Europe, North America and the northern parts of Asia an inhospitable frozen wasteland. Indeed, ice-sheet expansion and retreat has been a significant pattern for the past several million years, while before this cycle began the planet went through a much warmer phase. Many species, such as sabre-toothed tigers and woolly mammoths, have come and gone, and those that have survived have been those best able to adapt to these changing circumstances.

Forces that we are only just beginning to understand – caused, in the main, by the relationship between the Sun and the Earth – have driven these cycles of change. Man's impact upon this world, at least up until 100 years or so ago, has been negligible. But this is not true today, for now we are beginning to have a real influence on this globe, and much of it has been far from beneficial, driven by greed and mindlessness. What has been forgotten is that when we abuse nature we abuse ourselves.

Running parallel with the extensive exploitation of this planet by human activity is the growth of a new ecological awareness that seeks to stem the worst excesses of environmental degradation. This movement has achieved much, but a balance has had to be struck, for few people would want to relinquish the many benefits that science and modern society have brought into our lives. Is it, then, possible to have a harmonious, mutually beneficial relationship with nature? I believe so. This book shows how we can begin to connect with nature in a new way, and at the same time begin the task of rebalancing and clearing some of the subtle toxic effects our activity has inflicted on this planet.

My journey

My journey of exploration into the subtle energies of the Earth started in my childhood. I grew up within a family that believed in and practised spiritual healing. I recognised from a very young age that our thoughts have a powerful impact on our state of health and well-being, and that those thoughts can also influence and affect others. I used to love climbing trees, and would frequently visit a local forest to scramble up into these towering monarchs and sit nestled in their branches, enjoying the feeling of their solidity and power. I cannot claim that at that tender age I was aware of any consciousness within these trees – I just knew that I felt good when I was with them. This changed when I was in my early twenties and started to work consciously at developing my healing and intuitive skills. In this I was fortunate in having a number of very gifted teachers. I came to appreciate that consciousness runs through all life, and even those elements that we consider inert physical substances, such as the wind and water, hold patterns of consciousness within them. I began a dialogue with different beings within nature.

For the past 30 years I have explored these realms and have begun to appreciate the wisdom of this natural world and the amazing insights it can offer. There is so much that nature can teach us if we can but open our hearts to listen to the subtle messages that it has to impart.

I have come to recognise that there is a great desire within nature to cooperate and co-create with us to the mutual benefit of all living things upon this planet. This does not mean that we must forgo our technical devices, for all these things can be a part of nature's experiences too. It does not mean that we have to desist from cutting down any trees or harvesting crops from the land or from the oceans. It is not so much what we do but how we do it that is important. We have a choice – to act either tyrannically or cooperatively with nature. If we adopt the former mode, sooner or later nature will hit back – which, to an extent, it is already starting to do.

How to use this book

Working with Earth Energies will take you on a step-by-step journey, teaching you how to become aware of the subtle dimensions of nature and how to communicate with the different aspects of consciousness that imbue the natural world. This is not a difficult task but it does require a little patience and a willingness to listen.

The book will also teach you how you can begin to clear and rebalance energy problems that have been generated for the most part by destructive human activities. All thought, all emotion, leaves an energy imprint on the area where the experience occurred. In turn, others passing into that energy field are subtly affected by it. This is why homes take on a resonance that can generate happiness or unhappiness within their occupants. You will learn how to take a mental vacuum cleaner to the energies of your home, to spring-clean the patterns from the past and introduce a new dynamic quality to suit you.

Because energies affect us, it is important to learn how to protect oneself from their most destructive elements. For most people this happens at an unconscious level. Individuals who sit cross-legged and cross-armed are actually protecting themselves from resonant energies that cause them discomfort which is expressed in their body language. When clearing and rebalancing the energies of places, it is important to learn how to consciously create a shield that allows you to operate unhindered.

We can all make a difference

There are many ways in which we can individually make a positive contribution to this planet and influence some of the continuing problems that beset this world with our thoughts of balance and healing. Coming together in small groups can enhance this work, and this book shows how this can be successfully achieved. Group work is always a challenge yet the benefits are enormous, for it allows a greater level of creative energy to be generated and, when focused with conscious intent, can bring real benefits at both local and international level. Prayer in the form of balanced healing energy is truly a powerful tool in the arsenal of those who wish to consciously help human beings find a respect for each other and to heal the planet on which we live.

In recent years, through the inspiration of Jim Lovelock and his Gaia hypothesis* (which proposes that our planet functions as a single, self-regulating system in such a way as to maintain conditions suitable for life, just like any living organism), we have come to see this world as a conscious living entity. I know Lovelock would not quite go that far, at least not publicly, but from my perspective there is a level of conscious beingness that imbues this world which we might equate with Gaia. We might view such a being in the same way that the tiny microbes of our intestines view us. The consciousness of the Earth is on a very different level from our own, and yet we can still connect with it. We can be sure that the Earth will rid itself of human activity if we seriously threaten the stability of life on this planet, in the same way that we would cut out or destroy a cancer that was affecting our bodies.

Our challenge is to move away from being cancerous to being a benign partner working consciously with all aspects of creation. The more people who can do this the better it will be for the whole of humanity, for thought is infectious. The beliefs of the few today, if based on perennial truth, become the accepted concepts of the masses in the future.

In the mid-seventies I was responsible, with a small group of therapists, for setting up one of the first Natural Health Centres in the country in Cheltenham in Gloucestershire. We went on to found an organisation called the Natural Health Network which supported other centres wishing to establish complementary therapy

---

*Lovelock, J. E., *Gaia: A New Look at Life on Earth*, Oxford University Press (1979).

centres in their local towns. Twenty-five years down the road there are few towns that do not now have such a centre.

This explosion in the use of complementary therapies has been incredible. We have moved away from the cynical scepticism with which these systems were regarded in the mid-seventies to a wholesome respect for the many different ways in which health can be restored to the body. National newspapers now carry articles extolling the virtues of these various methods of treatment.

And so it can be for our relationship with the Earth. Nature is hugely resilient, as is illustrated by the speed with which environmental balance is restored after major oil spills and similar ecological disasters, such as the radioactive fallout from the Chernobyl nuclear power station in Ukraine. We can cooperate with nature in a most wonderful way if we open ourselves up to this possibility. It is a transformational process at a most profound level and brings benefits that touch every level of our being.

I recently heard a radio programme about a series of scientific studies carried out on the benefits of nature to our health and well-being. These studies showed that even a picture of some natural scene has a profound psychological effect on the people exposed to this image.

In one particular study a computer game was created with the sole intent of inducing anger and frustration in those who played the game. Groups of individuals were put in different rooms to play this game. One room had no pictures, another modern art paintings, another just one nature picture among a group of other paintings, and the fourth was filled with nature scenes. Health balances, in terms of blood pressure, pulse and emotional reactions, were monitored as the people played. The results were dramatic and startling. The frustration of those in the bare room was such that some individuals threw tantrums, and the same applied to the room with modern art paintings. But with only one nature picture in the room there was a measurable reduction in agitation and anger, while those who played the game fully exposed to nature scenes remained calm, clear-headed and able to circumvent their feelings as they worked their computers. These results and many similar studies demonstrate that nature heals, soothes and brings us positive benefits. This book will show you how to consciously draw on this sustaining healing energy.

We can only experience nature by being part of it. The separation process that has been part of humanity's quest over the past few thousand years may have been a necessary step in self-awareness, but it is now time to re-enter consciously the essence of nature, to link ourselves energetically with the Earth.

Our journey will involve different exercises for you to practise so that the concepts discussed here are not just another intellectual curiosity. Most of the exercises adhere to a standard pattern. In some instances you will need to be out in nature, but many can also be carried out within your own home.

The book is laid out in a coherent way that takes you step by step through different aspects of Earth consciousness, and is divided into two parts. Part 1 focuses on the many different dimensions that are part of our world, and shows how you can begin to communicate with the spiritual essences, such as those within trees, that imbue nature with life. Part 2 looks at what is meant by Earth energies and tackles in depth the various methods we can adopt in the healing of disturbed places. It will show you how you can participate in a unique way to bring healing and balance to this planet.

Throughout my thirty-five years practising as a healer and working with earth energies I have been blessed by support and help from a group of spiritual beings from beyond the physical world. This has gone hand in hand with the many dialogues that I have had with different life forms within nature. This higher guidance has been enormously helpful in clarifying and expanding concepts and ideas that I have struggled with. Nor have I been alone in this process, for other close colleagues have also added their insights and perceptions to this adventure. Without their enormous and valued input the coherence of ideas, in all that I convey through these pages, would be sorely lacking. What is presented through these pages is therefore a distillation from many different sources, all of which have added their contribution in many diverse ways. For this I am deeply grateful.

EARTH ENERGIES

Part 1

Chapter 1
Earth Consciousness

Why are we disconnected?

How many of us are truly aware of the spiritual dimension within nature? Sadly far too few, which is perhaps one reason why humanity can perpetrate such devastation on the Earth with so little regard to the cost of what is being done. There is no fault or blame apportionable in this, for we are what we are. Yet the consequences of what we do have far-reaching effects on our ever-so-adaptable Earth. We cannot continually pour greenhouse gases into the atmosphere without destabilising the climate. Global warming will inevitably lead to sea-level changes that will affect the whole planet. From time to time nature tries to remind us, sometimes in very dramatic ways, through hurricane, fire or flood, that it is time we woke up to what the Earth is all about. If we abuse nature through pollution and the destruction of habitats we are simply abusing ourselves, and such abuse inevitably leads to disease or imbalance at some level or another. It is an inescapable law. Reverse that process by learning to love and respect nature and we immediately become refreshed from an inexhaustible well of sustaining joy and vitality.

The mindless desire to exploit the Earth in every way is certainly fed by greed and materialistic concepts. Yet there may also be something deeper at work, for many sensitively aware and spiritually minded people often do not feel quite at home here. It is as though something is amiss in their connection with this planet, which can lead to feelings of physical discomfort. Such people often feel that their home is elsewhere and have a strong desire to move away from the Earth and all that it holds. This desire to escape is very strong and is evidenced in some religious teachings and beliefs, which suggest that the Earth is somehow evil or, at best, to be endured rather than loved and appreciated. But this is our home, we all belong here, and if we can truly align ourselves with its vibrant energies our lives will be filled with joy and happiness.

This book is all about showing you how to wake up to this other dimension in nature so that you can begin to communicate consciously with all that lies around you. Each expression of life on this planet has its own unique vibratory essence that embraces both its physical as well as its spiritual aspect. We are surrounded by a kaleidoscope of colour formed by a multitude of 'energetic resonances', each with its facet of consciousness, its inimitable character, playing its role in the dance of life. All is available to us if we are but willing to open ourselves to it.

The hidden dimension of nature

Think for a moment of a peaceful place in nature, a place that is special to you, either in the countryside or by the sea. It should be a place where you feel nurtured, or where its inherent beauty touches you in some profound way. Close your eyes and imagine yourself back in that scene, reliving the sights, sounds and smells that are all about you. Are you able to access your deeper feelings and to articulate why this place is so special to you?

This book is about accessing a subtle form of energy alive in nature. I will show you how to step into nature with a new level of awareness so that you can experience a deeper and more profound connection with the Earth and the natural world. You will learn how to tap into its energy, to experience its subtle qualities, leading you to a deeper level of appreciation and a more profound relationship with our planet. Each scene in nature is unique, vibrant and very much alive. Even in a desert, among the sand dunes, life exists whether we see it or not. Each scene has its particular tapestry of experience, its unique quality. It is this transcendent quality which reaches out to us when we begin to open up to receive what it has to offer.

At the core of life lie relationships – the relationships we have with our parents, our friends, our lovers, our enemies and, above all, our self are all part of the stream of experience that makes us who and what we are. The way we handle our relationships is a reflection of our inner essence, mirroring our strengths and weaknesses. By opening up to a new level of relationship with nature we dramatically deepen the well of our experience, allowing us to access new dimensions of our self; for there are energies in nature that are sublime, that can touch our souls at a most profound level. Because of this we cannot help but become more connected, more integrated as human beings, riding the waves of life with purpose, joy and a deep sense of fulfilment, so that when we meet storms and challenges we do so from a position of strength. In this we should not forget that the Buddha gained his enlightenment under a bo tree.

Now imagine again that you are back in your favourite place, but this time bereft of sight, hearing, sensation or smell. What, then, would you experience? Our logical minds would say nothing. But if you could begin to listen in another way, to listen with your heart, you might then begin to experience this other quality, this subtle dimension; which weaves through nature in a magical way. For reality, at this level, it is not just what we see, hear or encounter through our senses. What truly nurtures us when we step into nature is what we experience through our hearts and our souls. The following exercise will give you a sense of what I mean. I would suggest that with all the exercises given in this book you read them fully twice before carrying them out. You could also record them (a CD featuring the exercises can be obtained from the address given in the Appendix).

Opening the Heart Exercise
Aim: To open our heart energies
Time: 5 minutes

Find a place where you can sit comfortably and undisturbed. It is not necessary to adopt any particular posture, but in this instance, if you are used to meditating cross-legged in the lotus posture, that is fine.

1. Close your eyes and first become aware of your breathing. Try to feel that it is gentle and rhythmical.

2. Next focus on the area of your heart and imagine that over your heart there is a large flower. Any flower will do, but something like a yellow marigold or a pink rose would be ideal.

3. Try to imagine that the petals of the flower are fully open and you are now breathing through your heart, rather as though a stream of energy is flowing both into and from you through the flower over your heart.

4. What does this feel like? What sensations do you experience in your body?

5. Imagine you are in your favourite place in nature but now you are communicating through your heart. What do you sense and experience?

6. Finally thank nature from your heart and bring yourself back to full waking consciousness.

This exercise can be carried out inside, by imagining yourself in nature, or ideally out of doors in your garden, in a park or somewhere in the countryside. As with all exercises, practice helps, and I would suggest that henceforth when you step into nature you do so with a feeling that you are breathing through the flower over your heart.

Communicating with nature

By connecting to nature through your heart you will begin to sense a more profound level of connection with the Earth that can eventually lead to some of the most sublime feelings imaginable. It brings with it a deep sense of belonging and nurture; a sense of being truly at home on this most beautiful of planets.

This planet is unique in our solar system in its ability to provide a home for a whole range of life forms from the tiniest bacteria to the giant blue whales of the sea. When we step into nature we enter an environment that is vibrant with life. The trees, plants, birds, small animals, insects and microbes are all part of a web of experience whether we are conscious of those life forms or not. Nature is the living essence of all that is around us but includes rocks, streams, winds and the fiery expressions of lightning, volcanoes, fires and the heat of the Sun.

There are many ways in which we can consciously enter into these realms. A simple walk in the countryside, enjoying the sights, smells and sounds, can be a truly

nurturing, uplifting experience. But we can also add depth
to it, by learning to sense nature's subtle messages. In my
experience nature is alive and conscious at every level, and
it is quite possible to communicate with that consciousness in a variety of different ways, as this book will show.

There are four principal ways in which you can
communicate with nature:

- Through the sensations in your body
- Through your feelings
- Through verbal impressions sensed as an inner
  voice speaking to you
- Through clairvoyant images perceived within the
  mind's eye

Each exercise in the book will involve learning to access
information on these different levels. Because we are all
individuals we each need to discover the best way for us to
communicate with nature. For example, I find it easiest to
begin this communication process by first asking myself
'What do I feel?' when in any particular situation. If standing with my back to a tree, I will try to be aware of my
feelings before moving on to see what images or words
spring into my mind or what verbal messages I hear.
Others first get sensations in their bodies, such as a
tingling feeling in their back or on the top of their head,
before any clairvoyant impressions present themselves.

If you were to journey to a foreign country where
you met someone who could not speak your language, or
you his or hers, how would you begin to communicate?
Language is an ability common to all humans, but if
neither of you could speak you would have to resort to
other methods – sign language perhaps. If you persisted
and were patient, eventually you would learn how to
communicate in a way that was beneficial to you both. We
need to adopt the same approach with nature. Learning

new methods of communication will not come overnight unless you are very gifted; rather it will require patience and persistence.

Although you will learn a variety of techniques to help you communicate with nature, they all involve principally learning to listen to your inner voice, your inner knowing – your gut feelings – in a quiet, meditative way. When this is achieved the benefits are enormous, for not only will you then be able to conduct a dialogue with different species, such as trees, but also actively to draw on the wonderful healing benefits that nature bestows upon us.

The witch doctors of Madagascar

Many years ago I heard a talk given by a scientific researcher in Madagascar about the healing skills of the native witch doctors, who successfully used a variety of plants in many different ways in their therapeutic treatments. It is known that these people have not lived long on this island, and yet these witch doctors had an enormous repertoire of plants on which they regularly drew. When questioned about how they built up this knowledge they were amazed at the stupidity of the question. 'It is simple,' they said. 'We go into nature and ask the plants and they tell us!'

On another occasion I was sat with a Native American elder by a group of stones called the Whispering Knights, part of the Rollright stone circle group in Oxfordshire. After several minutes meditating by the stones he suddenly said that they had informed him that there was another standing stone nearby, which was connected to this group. Could we show him where it was? In this he was absolutely correct, for nearby but out of sight is another stone called the King's Stone. How did the stones communicate with him? The exercises in this book will show you.

Connecting with the Earth

Science tells us that everything is vibrating, is vibrating with its own unique essence. There are many energies on this planet that affect us, from physical forces like gravity to the more subtle manifestations from the spiritual realms of the Earth. We will look in turn at how each of these levels influence us, and how sacred sites, such as Mount Shasta in California or Glastonbury in England, have played a part in spiritual development. Over centuries some places have acquired immense power that can be used beneficially for healing. You will also be shown how you can begin to connect to these power centres in a more direct way, not only to help yourself but also to direct healing to different imbalances on the planet. Like us the Earth has its chakric or energy systems and its acupuncture points, for spiritual principles flow through all creation. We can learn to understand the Earth better by appreciating our connection with these different regions and sacred places.

To many people the physical structure of this planet – the rocks, water, wind and its fiery core – does not hold consciousness, or certainly not in the way that we recognise consciousness in animals or even plants. Yet mythology abounds with tales of the spiritual beings that inhabit our world. These are sometimes referred to as coming from the Faerie kingdoms or the realms of devas and elementals. I have had many dialogues with beings from these dimensions, and so have many of my friends and acquaintances. We are not experiencing a mass delusion but sharing something that is awesome in its implications, for these beings have much to teach us. Above all they can show us how to live in harmony on this Earth, and that alone is a wonderful gift.

To learn to communicate with these subtle entities you will need to believe in their existence. If you block your mind to their reality then you will never achieve the necessary sensitivity to their responses. I hope through these pages to present sufficient information to start you on a journey of exploration into the spiritual essences that weave through the physical domains of the Earth. It is quite possible to see, hear and sense what they have to offer us – not necessarily in a physical way, but certainly through our imagination.

Healing our environment

Now let us consider the opposite of a place where you feel the peace and tranquillity of nature. Think for a moment of somewhere you do not like, a place perhaps that generates feelings of fear, sadness or foreboding at some level. It might be a room in a house, an area of a town or even a place in the country.

What is it that causes these two so very different feelings – the peaceful, sustaining atmosphere of the first scene and the sense of disquiet of the second? Some aspects may be obvious, such as the architecture or the physical grouping of buildings, but others not so apparent.

Uncomfortable or disquieting feelings may be generated in very specific places, such as a corner of a room, while the rest of the house feels fine. Some places can feel cold, uninviting or even threatening. Nor is this restricted to buildings – some places in nature can also be imbued with a nasty heavy atmosphere. As wonderful as some places can be in uplifting our hearts and minds, so others can pull us down into the depths of our fears.

Home-owners know how necessary it is to take brush, broom or vacuum cleaner and physically to clean up dirt or dust as they accumulate. What is not generally appreciated is that our thoughts and emotions are particles of energy that flow out of us in a continuous stream and that these particles can also build up in different places and, in so doing, in a strange way, begin to take on a vibratory life of their own. Think for a moment of all of the thoughts and emotions that have flowed into your home from you, your family and perhaps its previous occupiers. A house that has had happy contented owners will always feel welcoming, while one that has witnessed emotional turbulence can seem uninviting. In most homes feelings of happiness are generally balanced by those of anger and frustration, giving a fairly neutral environment, but not in all cases.

As human beings we are very susceptible to subtle influences in our environment, which is why subliminal advertising can be so potent. What we seldom recognise is how much these small bundles of thought and emotional energy affect us. For spaces do hold energies from the past, and these most certainly can and do have an influence. A house that has experienced a deep trauma, such as the violent tensions involved in the break-up of a relationship, will be impregnated with this atmosphere. Subsequent occupants will often be sucked unwittingly into experiencing the same dynamics, and in some cases go on to replicate them. In recent years feng shui consultants have started to address this problem. We need to learn to tidy up both what we have created ourselves and, just as importantly, what has been left behind by others.

If you begin to think about the energy of your house in these terms, just imagine the impact of larger negative events, such as a war, on a given area. From my perspective, the hatreds that are still being generated in places like the Middle East are being continually fed by all the trauma that has accumulated from past generations. A soil steeped in blood will encourage bloodshed, particularly where strong feelings of hatred are involved. We only have to look at the recent example of the break-up of Yugoslavia into its different ethnic groups so see how thin is the veneer of civilised behaviour. So the other aspect of Earth consciousness this book seeks to address is that of healing the wounds of the Earth itself.

Healing the Earth

With conscious effort and goodwill, all Earth traumas caused by human activity can be corrected. However, the task of clearing all the mental and emotional mess that humanity has created, such as still exists in the ether of the Flanders battlefields or concentration camps like Belsen, will take future generations a very long time. What is encouraging at the moment is that more and more people are becoming conscious that there is something they can positively do, in a very real sense. They have begun the process of helping to heal the mental and emotional toxic energies that we have so liberally bestrewn over the Earth. This urgently needs to be tackled, and throughout this book different exercises will be given showing how it can be done in a safe and beneficial way.

The other aspect of Earth healing that needs to be addressed is our relationship with the planet. We need to find a new conscious relationship with the Earth, not just at an intellectual level but primarily through our bodies. The need to waken our inherent spirituality is important, but I would plead the case that it is vital to our long-term health and well-being on this planet that this spirituality is grounded fully in the physical; that in effect we spiritualise matter. Once this has been done we can truly align our physical self with the vibratory energy of the Earth in a process that brings great benefits on all levels and allows us to open to a new kind of Earth-centred spirituality. This is not difficult, and the exercise given at the end of this chapter will help you to begin to achieve this level of connection. It is a bit like learning to ride a bike; once the technique is mastered, it can be applied over and over again. These methods do need a little practice, but nature is awash with opportunities to help you develop these valuable and much-needed skills.

Consciousness in nature

I have been extraordinarily blessed in my life by having experienced directly what I will be sharing through these pages. I have been touched by nature in many different ways. To me, animals, trees, plants and even rocks are sentient beings with a consciousness that is very evident. It may seem bizarre to consider stones as having consciousness. Perhaps we all need to become a little crazy to venture into these realms; certainly there is a need to break out of the straitjacket of conventional thinking, to appreciate and embrace what might appear absurd with the openness of a child. We have to try to free ourselves from the limitations that upbringing and conditioning have imposed upon us. There have been many occasions when I have stood with my back to a tree, communicating with its essence and finding out about its rich and varied life. I have also communicated with rocks, crystals and simple stones, and there is much that I have learned from these dialogues. A rich imagination does help, but I know that something deeper is at work, that real communication is taking place. As in real-life conversations, I have been given information that I did not know at the time, could not possibly know, but was subsequently able to verify. I no longer need to convince myself, for the evidence for me has been overwhelming.

Nature's responses

It is a wonderful feeling to experience nature's responses, which can sometimes show themselves in quite dramatic ways. In the summer of 1993 I ran a week's inner development course on the Isle of Skye, which coincided with one of the major and rarely occurring planetary conjunctions of Neptune and Uranus. On the day in question the group of us who had gathered there decided that we would honour this event by holding a meditation up in the mountains of the Quirang.

Those who know Skye or the Western Isles of Scotland will be well aware how wet it can be here. This particular day was no exception. A dank, swirling mist infused with drizzling rain blotted out the hills and made our expedition decidedly uncomfortable. There were around twelve of us, and the journey to the place that was our destination required as much scrambling up steep slopes as more measured walking on well-trod paths. We eventually arrived, a fairly bedraggled group of meditators, at a flat area up in the mountains just before noon. All we could make out through the mist was the dark, jagged silhouettes of the rocks that surrounded us. We were alone in an eddying cloud of greyish whiteness, which paradoxically heightened our awareness, inducing strange feelings that we were being watched by many eyes peering at us through gloom.

How long did the meditation last? Perhaps five or ten minutes at the most, during which I made a deep connection with the 'spirit of the mountain' and the natural forces of that area. I closed my eyes in the mist and the dark and when I opened them again everything had been transformed; for the mist had vanished, the cloud had lifted and the sun was now shining brilliantly, presenting us with magnificent views out across the mountains and the glittering sea.

It was a breathtaking scene, and so extraordinarily unexpected. It was for me one of those defining moments in life, for in that instant I could no longer doubt. I had communicated in my meditation with the 'spirit of the mountain', sensing the subtle energies of all that was around me and giving thanks for what I was experiencing. There was joy in my heart, and when I opened my eyes I knew I had been answered. It is my sincere hope that this book will blow away the mists from your eyes so that you too can begin to experience the stunning vistas that are part of this real world.

Communicating with nature

Many people have now learned basic meditation techniques, how to still the mind and so on. Do not worry if you have not meditated before, for what is presented here will allow you to experience the benefits fully.

Meditation or Attunement Procedure
Aim: Basic meditation procedures
Time: 2–3 minutes

1. Begin all exercises by finding somewhere where you are comfortable and will not be disturbed. The main point of contact with the Earth is through your feet, and I would encourage you to adopt a posture in which your feet are on the floor or the ground, and not to sit cross-legged. We are in a process of needing to re-establish our connections with the Earth and not to disconnect from it, which is, in effect, what sitting cross-legged actually does at an energy level. I know that this can be hard if you are used to meditating cross-legged, but the effort is worth it.

2. Close your eyes and take a few deep breaths, trying to fully relax your body. With practice this need only take a few moments.

To my mind the exercise that follows is the most important that you will do. It can be practised time and time
again, and on each occasion your relationship with the
Earth will gain a new level. Like us, the Earth undergoes
its own evolutionary process that encompasses both physical as well as spiritual events and cycles. Many people are
aware that we are at a significant moment in its history,
when new vibrant subtle energies are streaming on to the
planet, inviting profound change at every level. Old structures are being broken down, demanding new ways of
being. Those who clutch fearfully and tenaciously to the
past, whether in religious or other institutions, are becoming locked into an ultimately self-destructive time warp.
They need help to let go of their fear and move with the
dynamics of these changing times. The Earth is going
through an amazing transformation, and we can and must
be part of this process; we need to continually reaffirm and
upgrade our connection with its vibrant energy.

   You do not have to do the whole exercise at any one
time; each step can be practised on its own. Indeed, I
would urge that you first work with steps 1–3, accessing
your inner light (even practising for two or three days),
before moving on to step 4, connecting with the Sun, and
then finally working with steps 5–8. Eventually it will
become a routine that can be invoked at will, in those
quiet times when you need to recharge your batteries, for
its self-healing properties are immense. You can practise
this exercise as many times as you like. Indeed, I would
suggest that you always precede any of the other exercises
in this book with this foundation exercise. With practice it
can be speeded up so that it does not take up too much
time. It will start the process of realigning your energies to
the vibratory rate of the Earth. In my experience human
beings are not innately aligned to the pulse of the Earth, so
this is a very important first step.

Earth Attunement Exercise

Aim: To connect energetically to the vibrational frequencies of the Sun and the Earth

Time: 5–10 minutes

Find a place where you can be quiet and will not be disturbed. Sit in a chair with your feet firmly placed on the floor. Do not sit cross-legged for this exercise, as your feet need to be in contact with the floor or, if possible, the ground outdoors.

1. Close your eyes and take a few breaths, relaxing your physical body, releasing any tension in your back, shoulders and neck.

2. Imagine that the inner essence of your being is represented by a point of light that resides somewhere within your body. It is most important that it is within you, not outside you. Some people initially sense this energy all around them, but for this exercise find its centre, its point of extreme focus. It does not matter whether you sense this light in your head, your throat, your heart, your solar plexus or your abdomen. Feel yourself connecting to its essence, becoming one with its luminosity.

3. Now think of the Sun and imagine that its magnificent energy is right over the top of your head. Imagine that a golden thread of light is coming from the Sun down through the top of your head and connecting to the light within you. What does this feel like? What do you experience?

4. Next direct this light down through your body and through the soles of your feet into the Earth. Imagine that the energy is penetrating deep into the ground, until it finally touches the very core of the planet. What do you sense lies within the 'heart of the Earth'?

5. Now imagine that this energy is returning to you, but this time see it as a colour that re-enters through the soles of your feet and fills the whole of your body.

6. Imagine that the colour from the Earth is entering your bones and that your skeleton is changing colour to match that coming from the Earth. Try to feel that the whole of your physical body is vibrating to this new pulse, particularly your bones. Bring your thoughts into the area of your heart and imagine that the energy of your heart is like a large pink or yellow flower. See its petals opening and sense that you are breathing energy in and out of your heart.

7. Become aware of all of the different parts of this exercise – the link to yourself, the link to the Sun, the link to the Earth and the opening of your heart. Try to feel that you are like a two-way transmitter of energy that connects the Sun to the Earth and back again.

8. Bring your thoughts back to your physical body and open your eyes, if possible maintaining the sense of this connection.

9. From time to time during the day think of these connections, for they will strengthen your energy links with the Earth.

In our journey so far we have considered that consciousness abounds around us wherever we are, and that each place exhibits a different quality of vibratory essence. We are affected by and affect all that we come into contact with, for we are in an inescapable realm of subtle energy exchanges. How conscious we are of these processes is our choosing, but with practice we can learn to be vastly more aware than we are at present for there is no limit to our awareness beyond what we choose to impose on ourselves.

Chapter 2
Subtle Energies

Before we can begin to explore nature in a new way we need to consider the energies that make up its subtle or hidden dimensions, for what we perceive at the physical level is but a tiny part of all that is held within these realms. Failing to make this connection is rather like trying to appreciate all the subtleties of a person's character simply from their photograph. We might make some perceptive assumptions, but it is only when we meet them face to face and then get to know them fully that we can begin to truly appreciate them as human beings. And so it is with nature, for it is only when we delve beneath the surface, to sense and connect with its subtle dimensions, that its full magnificence becomes apparent. Nor should we forget that we are ourselves part of nature, and can appreciate many of these aspects by looking at their reflection within us. As energetic beings we operate on many levels of experience encompassing these subtle domains.

Energy fields

To begin to recognise subtle energies we first have to consider what science understands energy to be. Every substance in the physical world is an expression of the electromagnetic spectrum, which contains different wavelengths of pulsating energy. This spectrum includes light, sound, microwaves and X-rays, as well as all the atomic substances that make up our physical universe. Objects that appear solid to our touch are primarily space, held together in a lattice of vibrating atomic particles. It is sometimes hard to see ourselves as miniature universes primarily made up of space but that, at one level, is what we are. Energy, from a scientific perspective, is the movement of forces within the electromagnetic spectrum. It is defined as: *'a quantity that describes the capacity to do work; commonly divided into three major classifications: kinetic (dynamic) energy, potential (static) energy, and radiant (electromagnetic) energy'.*[†]

Electromagnetic fields weave through the physical world in a seamless web connecting particle to particle. These energy fields surround and permeate all living things, creating slightly different matrices of energy depending upon the organism in question. Physical fields, such as heat radiation and gravitational fields, also extend out from physical bodies in haloes of energy which can be detected by scientific equipment.

The subtle dimensions

Running parallel to this electromagnetic spectrum is another range of energy frequencies or subtle energies which are non-physical and therefore cannot be detected by normal scientific means. Spiritual healing and telepathy are two examples of non-physical subtle energy. In recent years Professor Robert Jahn at Princeton University has carried out thousands of experiments showing how the mind alone is able to influence a random electronic generator by just willing the equipment to act one way or

[†]http://www.academicpress.com/inscight/03191997/energy1.htm

another. This is another example of the use of subtle
energy but, because it lies outside the electromagnetic
spectrum, science has had a hard time accepting the validity of these experiments. These energies are not part of the
electromagnetic spectrum and therefore, in scientific
terms, are not considered energy. Nevertheless, subtle
energies display all the hallmarks of how energy works
according to the definition given above. One way to
approach an understanding of subtle energy is to consider
how it operates within us.

I am sure you are fully aware of your physical body,
although when it is functioning well you might sometimes
take it for granted. I hope also that you are aware of your
spirit, or at least have a sense that there resides within you
a unique spiritual essence or individual life force. We can
therefore say that there are two distinct parts of your
make-up.

1. **Your spirit**, which is eternal and can operate outside
   the space–time continuum.

2. **Your physical body**, which is mortal and is held
   within the space–time continuum.

For these two parts to work in balance together there has
to be a bridge or means of communication between the
two. If not, life would become impossible. So how does
your spirit communicate with your body, and vice versa?

There is continuous energy exchange between your
spirit and your body. When this breaks down at any level
your health becomes impaired. One way this flow of energy
can be understood is by using the metaphor of a piano,
with the bottom or bass octave representing the physical
self and the top or treble octave the spiritual. Imagine that
you are such a piano with the bottom octave representing
all the energies of your physical body and the top octave
the energies of your spiritual self. All the intermediate

octaves, representing your emotions, your mind, your ego, your chakric energies and so on, are, in effect, all part of the subtle energy aspects of yourself. Now something very interesting happens when any note of the piano is sounded, for a vibration is set up in the string that causes all similarly pitched notes to vibrate. For example, if you were to play the note middle C, the vibration in the string would set up a pulse that would be transferred to every other C note on the piano – each octave of the C note, from the bottom to the top, would vibrate.

The simple principle to be grasped is that energy is exchanged through resonance when two things are of the same frequency, such as middle C and its counterparts in other octaves. This is why our emotions and thoughts affect the body, and conversely why substances that we put into our body, such as sugar, alcohol or caffeine, affect our mind and feelings. It is for this reason that higher or finer frequencies can translate down to the physical level – for example, when spiritual healing is practised.

From this analogy you can see that whatever you do at a physical level creates a vibration that transfers energy across octaves to the spiritual part of you. Likewise any thought or emotion that flows from your consciousness causes a vibration that affects your physical body. There is a dance of energy going on within us the whole time. Exactly the same process happens within every living organism, although in simpler organisms, such as bacteria, fewer octaves are involved.

The bridge between the physical body and the next octave up, which is sometimes called the etheric body, is at the quantum level. Science is now aware of how particles of matter can appear and disappear contrary to the normal laws of physics. This is the boundary between the physical and non-physical worlds. In this context we normally think of the spiritual aspect as vibrating on a very high frequency and the physical aspect on a dense, low frequency. Figure 1 shows this step-down of energy across octaves. This is one aspect of subtle energy as it operates within us.

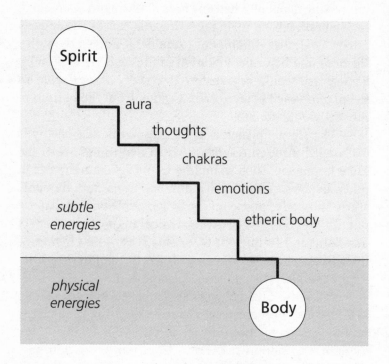

Fig. 1 Energy transfer within the body

Over time different subtle energy fields have been given names that describe their quality and patterning. The aura is the sum total of all the subtle energy fields that surround the body. It reflects the thoughts and emotions of the person but also has an important role, like the Earth's atmosphere, in detuning destructive subtle energy influences which might upset the balance of the organism. The chakras are gateways of energy that link these fields (octaves) together.

Resonance

To understand these processes in more depth, let us suppose that you and a few of your friends decide to meet up regularly once a week for a meditation evening. One of the members has a room that is not being used for other purposes so you all agree to redecorate it in suitable colours and then dedicate the room exclusively to your special sessions. Over a period of time you begin to establish a real harmony between you, and you discover that the group dynamic considerably helps the quality of your meditations. This is because resonating subtle energy accumulates when people come together. These energies, as long as they are in harmony, give everyone a lift, which is why meditating in a group can be much easier than meditating alone.

While you are meditating together a web of connecting energy is built up between you, which unites everyone energetically. Again there is a simple but important principle to be understood here. When two or more 'energies' come together with the intention of connecting, a resonance is created which starts to build a bridge between them, allowing energy to flow. This can again be understood in musical terms. If you were to hold a tuning fork pitched at C and your friend played the corresponding C on a piano then your tuning fork would start to vibrate in resonance with the pulse of that sound. On a subtle level, if you send out energy from yourself, such as a healing thought to a friend, the transmission of that energy is like playing one of the notes on the piano and will cause the corresponding note within your friend to vibrate also. This is the basis of telepathy, for distance is no barrier at this level and connections can be made instantly across the planet.

When two people come together, different facets of subtle energy are transferred between them. Now no two people vibrate in exactly the same way. All our pianos, so to speak, are slightly differently tuned, which is why adjustments have to be continually made. When a powerful connection is created, people will often unconsciously mirror each other's actions as a form of non-verbal communication. When a group comes together for meditation, a vibratory note, or more accurately a series of notes, is established to which individuals consciously or unconsciously will try to attune themselves. This does not happen overnight but takes time and practice. It is like singing a note that becomes purer and purer which you all seek to replicate within yourselves.

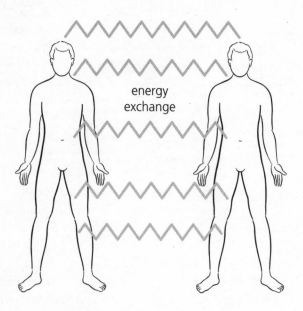

energy exchange

Fig. 2 Subtle energy exchange between people

As each person develops their awareness, so the quality and depth of the meditations will increase – the notes become finer, or take in more octaves (for these are infinite), and this, in turn, has a heightening effect on the energy of the room.

Let us suppose that you start to carry out some healing work at the end of your meditation session. This will add another set of frequencies to the energy in the room. Indeed, the more ambitious the work the more potent the energies will become until eventually they start to take on a life of their own.

Discordant energy

Energies that bring harmony and healing will always uplift people, but not all energies fall into this category. Most individuals will have experienced disturbed energy at different times in their life, and the more sensitive you become the more this can be a problem. Disturbed energy normally has the effect of metaphorically putting your piano out of tune and consequently breaking down your ability to function coherently. An example of this might be when you are in the line of fire of an individual who has become very angry, for the energy they give off can be almost as devastating as physical violence. Most people will feel this disturbing energy as a punch in their solar plexus region, sometimes making them feel physically sick.

Resonant energy also runs through groups of people with a collective intent, such as a football crowd, and can on occasions be so potent as to cause individuals to act in uncharacteristic ways. Many cases of mob violence are fuelled by negative subtle energies that have insidiously driven the collective will.

Creating subtle energy

Let us return to the meditation group. After a year of meeting together one of your friends has the offer of a job in another part of the country and is obliged to move away. Giving some thought to the situation, you agree to open up the vacancy to a mutually known psychic friend.

The first time the new person attends your group they are immediately aware of the atmosphere in the room and comment on its beautiful quality.

What has happened to the room in the space of those twelve months? Remember those tiny packets of emotional and mental energy, mentioned in Chapter 1, that are continually flowing from us. We might call them bundles of subtle energy. When we come together in a group meditation there is a focus of mind and intention, which adds a very specific quality to these subtle energies. Effectively you have been filling the room with a particular quality of energy, the strength of which triggers the response in your new member.

There are two aspects that need to be borne in mind at this stage.

1. The subtle energies we are discussing here are not electrical charges, nor do they relate to the electro-magnetic spectrum in any way. Physical energies can change in strength but not in quality.

2. Subtle energies have their unique characteristics. For example, each emotion, such as love, peace, anger, hatred, joy, happiness, produces a corresponding subtle energy. Subtle energies can change in quality as well as strength.

Returning to the group meditation analogy, depending upon the techniques you used the room would start to take on the essence of whatever was the focus of your meditations. For example, you might decide always to include an exercise of visualising a lotus flower in the centre of the room. This symbol is widely used by meditators across the world, and when you think of a lotus in this way something else magically happens.

Accessing collective energies

Over hundreds of years people have been meditating on the lotus, creating packets of subtle energy that reflect the inner state of calm that they have been able to achieve. These thoughts do not simply disappear but continue to exist for a very long time. It is rather like throwing a pebble into a pool – the ripples go on for ever. So as well as imbuing their meditation rooms with these energies these people are also feeding a collective pool of energy that is part of humanity's heritage. These energies are then available for anyone to draw upon.

By simply thinking of a lotus in a meditative way you immediately connect with all the accumulated thought patterns around the lotus. And every time you meditate on the lotus you add a tiny bundle of energy to that collective pool. It is just like using an icon in a computer to access a particular programme. So by meditating on the lotus over a period of time a lotus-specific energy of inner peace and tranquillity (think of the serene features on the face of the Buddha) would build up in the room, because of your meditations but also fed by the subtle energy of all those other people who have meditated upon the lotus held within the collective psyche of humanity. This is why meditating upon widely used symbols can be a great help in your meditations, for you are aligning yourself with the subtle energies that they hold.

The following exercise will give you a sense of what I am talking about.

Lotus Attunement Exercise
Aim: Learning to communicate with the energy of the lotus
Time: 10–15 minutes

Have a look in a book for a picture of a lotus (if you cannot find a lotus a water lily will do), so that

you can more easily visualise its image. Adopt the
usual position of meditation given in Chapter 1, close
your eyes and relax.

1. First of all connect to your inner light, as described
in the exercise on p. 18, and feel its energy flowing
through the whole of your body.

2. Next imagine that a lotus flower is over the top of
your head, exuding peace and calmness, being aware
that you are linking energetically to a symbol that has
been used for thousands of years. What sensations do
you experience in your body? Can you feel its
serenity and tranquillity? If not, what other feelings
do you get?

3. Try to imagine that the lotus is speaking words to
you. What messages do you get in your mind?

4. See whether any other images come to you,
whether you start to gain picture impressions, which
are also messages on another level. For example, you
might see a tranquil scene in nature.

5. Now bring the image of the lotus down to the area
of your heart and repeat the process that you used for
the head, but this time feel that it is your heart that is
receiving the connection and communication. Note
any differences that you experience.

6. Next, when you have completed the connection
with the heart, bring the lotus down under your feet
and feel that it is connecting you to the Earth through
its roots. Go through the same procedure that you
have already enacted with the head and the heart,
noting once more anything that you experience.

7. Finally, slowly disconnect from the lotus, bringing
yourself back to full waking consciousness.

You can break this exercise down into separate
sections – head, heart and under your feet – if this
makes it easier for you.

Build-up of energy

The next concept that needs to be appreciated is that
subtle energy accumulates over a period of time. The more
a meditation room is used, the greater the potency of its
atmosphere becomes. These energies last for a very long
time, rather like the half-lives of radioactive isotopes,
which is why sacred places from the past can still be very
powerful today. Any other person who then uses the meditation room will immediately receive a psychic boost to
their meditations or healing work. The same applies when
you use a particular place for your own meditations and
attunements, although generally one person on their own
cannot generate as much energy as two or three people
gathered together.

All human activity produces similar patterns. Places
that have been used for torture carry all the pain and fear
that these terrible acts have generated. This is why there is
such a pall over places like Belsen. The negative subtle
energies that have been built up there are of a very high
level of intensity. To be cleansed they will need to be
tackled by subtle energy of equal potency. And this brings
us to another very important point. Subtle energy will
always flow from the stronger force to the weaker, just as
in the laws of physics. If you wired two batteries together,
one of six volts and the other of twelve, there would only
ever be a one-way flow between the two, from the twelve-
volt to the six-volt.

From these comments you might suppose that a
crowd of 100 people would generate far more power than
a group of six. In theory, yes, but another significant factor

needs to be borne in mind. The quality and strength of the energy are also affected by the degree of harmony or clarity of intent within a group. I cannot stress enough the importance of the need to create group harmony when meditating or carrying out any collective psychic work, and will return to this theme again later in the book. I know from experience that it takes many meetings for real harmony to be established, and the more people are involved the harder that process becomes. So six people, working in real harmony with focused intent, can often produce a more potent force, like a laser, than several hundred whose 'energies' are slightly at odds.

The same principle can be applied to any group activity, whether in a religious organisation or a limited company. If a group has a clear mission and a willingness to work in harmony together they will achieve amazing things.

Group dynamics

The success and power of any group are dependent on the degree of love and harmony that you can develop between you. This is very subtle and quite difficult to describe, because real harmony has to be experienced in order to be recognised. I have attended groups as a guest where there has been good harmony between members and others where the harmony has been sadly lacking, despite protestations to the contrary. You should aim for a state where it is possible to share what you are feeling and experiencing quite openly, without any fear of being criticised. This requires a considerable degree of trust. Energetically you will also need to work on finding a harmonious balance. The following is an exercise that will help you achieve this.

Creating Harmonious Energy within a Group
Aim: To stabilise and balance the energies of a group
Time: 10–15 minutes

You will need to come together in your usual group meeting place. I would suggest that you sit around in a circle and that someone leads you through the stages of this meditation.

1. Everyone should close their eyes and carry out the exercise for linking to the Sun and the Earth given in Chapter 1 (see p. 18).

2. Next connect to your inner light, as described in Chapter 1 (see p. 17), but this time imagine that it has a particular colour that reflects you.

3. Imagine that you are sending out this coloured energy from your solar plexus region in a clockwise direction around your circle, so that you are creating ribbons of different-coloured energies within the group.

4. Very slowly in your mind try to blend your energy with that of the other people so that the colours start to merge. This will need to be practised, but eventually you will find that they blend together to create a white light.

5. When this white band of light has been established, continue the process of blending the energy and then take the vibration up to a slightly finer level. You can do this by imagining you are bringing sunlight into the room and everything is getting lighter and brighter.

6. You will find when you do this that the energy within the group will start to waver, for not everyone will be able to do this in synchronisation.

7. After holding this finer level for a few minutes, bring the energy frequency back down to the level it was at before by imagining that it is getting heavier.

Practice will be required, and this can only be achieved by a sense of commitment to the group dynamic, which is why smaller groups of six or less generally work best. In any circumstances I would not normally want to work with a group of more than twelve people, which I would see as the maximum for effective work because of the difficulty of creating real harmony. I would urge you to continue practising these types of exercise, as they will start to establish a firm platform on which you can build.

Protection

Before looking at how to attune ourselves to different aspects of the natural world and to sacred sites, something needs to be said about psychic protection and why it is important.

Why do we need to protect ourselves? As has already been stated, all activities create bundles of subtle energy, each with their own characteristics and quality. Not all these energies are uplifting and healing, and when you consciously interact with a known sacred site by attuning to its energies you potentially open yourself up to all that has taken place there.

Even if a sacred site, such as Stonehenge, has been used for healing and spiritual work, it does not mean to say that everyone who has been there has been in a healthy, balanced mental state. Individuals carrying murder and hatred in their hearts might also have tried to interact with its energies, particularly if the site has been in existence for a very long time. In some cases ritual human sacrifices might have taken place, especially if the site originated or was used in Celtic times. The same is true of many Central American sites.

We need to ensure that we access pure spiritual energy untainted by any negative overlay, and the only way we can do this is by creating a shield around ourselves. If you omit this aspect then sooner or later you will experience a negative reaction, causing you to feel drained of energy or even become physically sick.

Sometimes individuals challenge me by saying that people who protect themselves do so only because they are frightened. If they are frightened of something then they simply attract that thing, whatever it is, to themselves. There is some measure of truth in this statement, for fear is an energy that can easily pull us down. Ultimately we have to confront our fears. So yes, if you are frightened of something, you will attract it to yourself. However, my response to the question is to ask the person 'Why are you wearing clothes?' If you think about it we wear clothes to protect ourselves from changes in climate – it is as simple as that, and has nothing to do with fear.

When venturing into the exploration of subtle energies we need to appreciate that some of these energies can potentially be very destructive. To become aware of these finer dimensions we have to develop our sensitivity, rather like turning up the volume of our inner radio set to be able to hear some of the very faint channels. But what happens when we turn the dial and pick up a channel that is broadcasting from nearby? The blast of sound from the speakers can be excruciating if we have not first turned down the volume. We need therefore need to create a form of protection that allows us to adapt to different environmental circumstances.

It is also important, as I have said before, to recognise that, as a principle, energy will always flow from the stronger force to the weaker. Tune into or connect yourself with an energy that is stronger than you and you will be swamped by that energy. If it is a beneficial energy, all well and good, but if it is not then you have a problem.

These are the simple laws of science transferred to another level. Protection is a very necessary part of physical experience, and most species employ some form of it. You would not last very long if your immune system did not fulfil a very valuable function in maintaining your health. Fear has very little to do with this natural self-defence mechanism.

Methods of protection

Protection Exercise 1
Aim: To learn how to protect yourself energetically
Time: 5–10 minutes

Find a place where you can be quiet and will not be disturbed and then carry out the attunement exercise given in Chapter 1.

1. Close your eyes and connect to your inner light which you discovered in the first exercise. Feel and imagine this light becoming brighter and stronger, and sense its energy extending out from your body until this bubble of light completely surrounds you. Make sure that it is under your feet as well as over the top of your head and around your back.

2. Once you have made your connection to the Sun, ask the Sun to send the right energy to you for protection. I would like you to imagine that you have three choices – a white, a sky-blue or a golden ray, which all hold protective qualities. Whichever feels right, see or sense this energy flowing around the outside of your inner light bubble, as though you were adding an extra layer to it.

3. Now imagine that this additional layer is gently spinning around you in a clockwise direction.

4. Bring yourself back to full waking consciousness, but still sense that this protective bubble of energy is enveloping you, gently spinning all the time as you go about your daily tasks.

5. From time to time during the day, close your eyes for a few moments and reinforce the visualisation, by sensing this coloured light spinning around you, shielding you from any negative energies.

Practising this exercise on a regular basis, like an athlete training for competition, will help you create a strong protective energy field around you. It will make it easier for you when needing to call on your protection when accessing the energies from sacred sites or power centres.

There are many systems that we can adopt to protect ourselves when attuning to the energies of sacred sites or carrying out any landscape healing work. Some of you may already be using different psychic protection methods, and if they work adequately for you then do continue to use them. What I am suggesting here is suitable for those who are new to these experiences.

There are two aspects that need to be practised when venturing into working with subtle energies. The first is the need to protect oneself and the second is learning to put protection around someone or something else. You can protect your family as well as your car or your meditation room, and all three might be necessary at different times.

You might like to experiment with using the three suggested colours other than the one you have chosen for yourself. In other words, if you chose gold, see what it feels like when you use white or sky-blue protection. All these colours are linked to primary archetypal energies that carry a protective element. Gold is associated with a yang or masculine element of the Sun, blue, like the cloak of the Madonna, connects to the universal feminine, and white is a reflective energy symbolising purity that blends both masculine and feminine qualities. As we are all individuals some colours suit us better than others.

To reinforce the strength of your protection, you should practise the exercise frequently. Eventually you will be able, in just a few moments, to create a strong protective force which will allow only beneficial energies to flow into you in a measured way, and will repel or defuse those forces that are destructive. As with all forms of agility and athleticism, it is practice that counts.

Protection Exercise 2
Aim: To learn how to put protection around another person or object
Time: 5–10 minutes

For this exercise you will need a lighted candle in front of you, either on the floor or on a small table.

1. Adopt your usual posture for meditation, then put protection around yourself.

2. Carry out the Earth Attunement Exercise given in Chapter 1, but keep your eyes closed.

3. Now imagine that you are projecting the energy of your protective colour out through your hands and surrounding the candle. It is important that you still sense your own protection around you and that this new protection for the candle is in the form of an additional bubble of light.

4. Visualise this protective light also spinning around the candle. How long are you able to hold your concentration in this exercise?

5. You can break for a few minutes to give yourself a rest, and then repeat the exercise, this time with your eyes open.

6. Finally imagine that the protection around the candle is growing larger and larger until it finally encircles the whole room. You now need to feel that not only are you within your own individual protection but you are also within the spinning protection you have created around your room.

7. Hold this thought for several minutes if you are able, and then bring yourself back to full waking consciousness and open your eyes.

Again, you will need to practise this exercise regularly, eventually extending it to include putting protection around your whole house and then around other objects that might be vulnerable in some way. As with the candle, you can project these protections over a distance. Indeed, distance is no barrier; for example, if one of your family members is backpacking around the world you can place protection around them wherever they are by imagining them in place of the lighted candle.

If you have a friend with whom you can practice these exercises, then so much the better. You can try putting protection around each other and seeing how it feels. Is it comfortable? If not, then ask yourself what you need to do to adjust the energy in some way so that it becomes satisfactory.

Finally, two things need to be borne in mind. First, by connecting to the Sun and the Earth you have effectively asked for guidance and help from two incredibly powerful yet loving sources of conscious support, for both will link you through to profound spiritual realms. These forces will never let you down and will always provide you with the answers to any questions that you might have. You might not want to hear these answers but they are there nonetheless. Second, if you wish to make a connection with any other source of spiritual support and protection, then feel free to do so. We all come from different cultural and spiritual backgrounds and we need to find those qualities that are in true resonance with our self.

Chapter 3

Sacred Sites and Power Centres

In this chapter we will consider the ways in which you can begin to explore the energies within nature, looking particularly at those places that are regarded as sacred sites, and how you can begin to access some of the energies within 'power centres'. Connecting to places already regarded as special will help you begin the process of becoming more aware of the subtle dimensions within nature. This is not something that will necessarily happen overnight, but each step will help you deepen your connection with these amazing energies.

Sacred sites

Sacred sites fall into two categories:

1. Those that derive their energy from nature.
2. Those that have been created by people.

Holy mountains such as Mount Shasta in northern California or Ayers Rock (Uluru) in Australia, and sacred streams and healing wells such as the 'Holy Well' in Malvern, England, fall into the first category. In fact, from my perspective all of nature is a sacred site, but certain places have, over a long period of time, gained a reputation for some extra quality or dimension, in some cases becoming centres of pilgrimage. Once they are imbued in this way human collective consciousness will add its legacy to the place in question. The meditation that we carried out on the Isle of Skye, mentioned in the first chapter, would have added an extra quality or dimension, however small, to the site in question, so that others, coming to the same place to meditate or attune, would in principle be able to pick up something of our energetic experience. In this sense there are very few places that have not been exposed in some way or another to human contact. Indeed, once a place achieves the accolade of being called a 'sacred site', by definition it becomes infused with human psychic energy. There is nothing wrong with this as long as individuals are aware of what is taking place.

How does a natural site come to be sacred?

Some places have stunning views or capture some particularly beautiful feature, but in most cases it is the vibratory quality of the spiritual essence or consciousness of the particular place which provides the attraction. This is sometimes called the 'genius loci', the presiding deity or spirit of a place. When sites take on the mantle of being sacred, human contact with these spiritual essences is established and forms of communication can take place. In the experience on Skye mentioned in Chapter 1, my communication with the 'spirit of the mountain' was in effect a contact with the 'genius' of that place. On occasions a site might become sacred because of an apparition, such as the appearance of the Madonna at Lourdes in France, or the sighting of the archangel Michael at St Michael's Mount in Cornwall.

Some places also hold special qualities because of their physical make-up. The high iron content of the spectacular hills around Sedona in Arizona is a case in point, although here other levels of energy are involved that stem from an etheric race of beings that once resided on our planet in the distant past. The high quartz crystal levels in rocks such as granite produce a small electrical discharge, which it is claimed heightens awareness. It is interesting how many stone circle sites in the UK, such as Avebury, are built of rocks with a high quartz content; the granite King's Chamber in the Great Pyramid of Giza is another such example. But in most cases it is the genius of the place that creates its special quality.

Man~made sites

Sacred sites created by human beings are many and varied. Any place that has been used for spiritual work can be classified in this way. The degree of potency of the place will be dependent upon how long the power has been actively generated. An Egyptian temple such as that dedicated to the goddess Hathor at Denderah in Egypt holds power far in excess of what would be found in a modern church, but not necessarily greater than that found in, say, a Tibetan monastery. From this it might seem that we should always seek out established sacred sites for our spiritual work, but in this there is a catch. Any place used extensively for spiritual activity can help the aspirant make a more profound connection with the spiritual planes. But such a connection will always be constricted in some way or another because of the particular slant of the religious group or organisation originally associated with the site. Tune into an Egyptian temple and you will get Egyptian-quality energy, which will be different from that of a Greek temple and different again from that of a Bronze Age stone circle in Britain. Each has its own essence, its own unique quality. The trick is to seek out those places that are in harmony with us and to draw on their particular subtle energies.

It is also interesting to speculate on why certain places have been chosen in the past as the sites of temples or other sacred sanctuaries. Undoubtedly some have been chosen because of their obvious connection with the natural world, such as the sacred groves of the Druids. But others could have been chosen for more practical reasons, such as proximity to a town or city.

From my researches into the megalithic long barrow sites of Wessex, which are more than 5,500 years old, it is clear that these have been set out in a geometric pattern that straddles the landscape. Each placement had to be where it is because of its geometric relation to its neighbour. What is interesting here is that the establishment of such a site immediately starts to create a connection with the Earth and its subtle energies. This phenomenon has been noted by dowsers and has generated much speculation, along chicken-or-egg lines, as to whether the site creates the energy matrix, including attracting underground water, or whether it was built where these patterns were already established.

My own experience suggests that a sacred site could be created in the most abysmal area, and that the very act of its creation would change the energy frequencies of the place. Indeed, if you were to create a sacred space in your garden you would attract to it all the healing and beneficial energies of nature.

The power of place

Accessing the subtle energies of places with great power provides a very valuable boost to one's inner development, but it is also important not to get locked into the past. This can be achieved quite easily now because of our access to a transport system that can move us around the planet in a matter of hours. We can, with few exceptions, easily visit different sacred sites across the planet, and in so doing experience a much wider range of spiritual energies than was available in past times.

The Earth is constantly absorbing new spiritual energies, which have the effect of breaking down many of the old structures that have served us so well in the past. We have to be open to flowing with these exciting fresh energies; to learn and draw from the past yet without being constrained by it.

Different sacred site energies

Sacred sites come with many different qualities of energy, dependent upon how they have been established and subsequently used. Those sites that stem from nature will always carry a quality that reflects the 'genius' of the place. And, as already stated, each place will be overlaid with other energies arising from human activity. Well-known sites generally have a very broad range of frequencies.

Sites created by human beings can often be much more specific. For example, the temples of Egypt and Greece, devoted to one or other of the gods or goddesses, will reflect this explicit connection. To visit a site dedicated to a particular archetype, like the temple of Apollo at Delphi in Greece or the Egyptian goddess Isis at her temple at Philae in Egypt, will provide an opportunity to access the distinct quality of energy that stems from the relevant archetype.

A living example can be found today in the Hindu temples of India, which are dedicated to different gods and goddesses of the Vedic pantheon. Broadly speaking, mosques, synagogues and Christian churches have a more universal quality, reflecting their beliefs, although in the case of the latter the dedication to a specific saint will add its own influence. Moreover, many churches have been built on much older sacred sites, so a whole range of different 'energies' may be involved.

The stone circle sites of Britain were established in groups, with each site having a particular task or function. Some, like the Trippet Stones on Bodmin Moor in Cornwall, were used for healing the landscape; others, like the Duloe Circle, again in Cornwall, for connecting to star energies; some, like the Stanton Drew stone circle in Somerset, were used for monitoring the balance of energetic patterns across the planet so that corrections could be made when imbalances were detected, and so on. As might be appreciated, such conclusions have come from my inner connection with these places, and not from any archaeological evidence, which generally tells us very little about the use of these sites. It is an endless list, because there are so many different ways in which the subtle energy from these centres can be used.

Self-healing and sacred sites

As shown in Chapter 1, the simple act of visiting a sacred site and opening up through your heart to its subtle energies will invariably cause inner movement and growth. You cannot energetically touch such places without being transformed by them. In this respect it is important to remember that sometimes such transformations can be challenging. You will unblock stagnant energies in yourself, and the transformation can sometimes be radical. In the process of spiritual growth it is often important to let go patterns of behaviour that are no longer appropriate.

I frequently take groups to Egypt because many people sense a connection with this amazing ancient civilisation, which lasted for several thousands of years. The energies that stemmed from this culture can be used in many different ways. The temples offer places where it is possible to connect with a very powerful focus of specific energies, so that an individual who feels a resonance with, say, the energy of Horus will find this in his temple at Edfu. But despite all its great achievements, Egypt also had its darker side, and sometimes deeds were carried out that caused trauma to individuals. I have worked with people on these trips who have felt they had a past life in Egypt during which some problem occurred. Visiting these places provides an opportunity to release blocked energies that have been held deep within the psyche. Simply being there with an openness to change will release much of what has been locked away for many years.

Working with the energy of sacred sites

You have many options as to how to connect with the energy of a sacred site. At the simplest level just visiting a place and drinking in its vibrational quality may be all that is necessary for you. Many travel to places like Glastonbury and Avebury in the UK, or simply to some well-known local site or beauty spot, just for this purpose. The value of this cannot be over-estimated. But you may wish to access the energy in a more direct way to assist with healing or Earth energy work, and this is where power centres come into their own.

Before we look at how we can use the energy of such places in a more direct way, the following exercise will help you begin to connect with the energies of a sacred site.

Sacred Site Attunement Exercise
Aim: Learning to attune to the energy of a sacred site
Time: 15–20 minutes

To carry out this exercise you will need to find a sacred site in your locality. It does not have to be a well-known place; indeed, any especially beautiful place will do.

1. Begin your exercise by first putting protection around you as described in Chapter 2. You will need to do this before you reach the site – spending a few moments of attunement before accessing the place will be very beneficial.

2. When you arrive, walk around the area, monitoring what feelings and sensations arise within you. Try to sense whether any particular area has a special quality that makes it different from the rest.

3. Find a place where you can sit on the ground and close your eyes, then carry out the Earth Attunement Exercise given in Chapter 1.

4. Ask the Sun for help and then attune to the subtle energy of the site by asking the following questions:

a. What sensations do I experience in my body, such as heat or cold, or tingling sensations in my feet, head, arms or back?

b. What feelings do I get from this place, such as calmness, anger, peace, and so on?

c. If I imagine that this place is speaking to me, what messages do I get?

d. What picture images come to my mind when I connect with the subtle energy of this place?

5. Disconnect from the energy, slowly bring yourself back to full waking consciousness and open your eyes. Make sure that you feel grounded within your body by being aware of the sensation of the ground beneath your feet.

Whenever you visit a sacred site or intend to carry out some energy work, first put up your protection. I cannot stress this enough. In some places you will feel strong healing energies, and it is quite in order to draw on these to help you find full health and balance in your life.

Power centres

We now come to the more complex issue of power centres. In many ways what follows overlaps with what we have discussed concerning sacred sites. The distinction with power centres lies in the intention of wanting to draw upon the particular energy of the place and direct it consciously to help balance specific situations on the planet.

The primary way in which power centres are created is through groups of people coming together for spiritual purposes. There are many such centres that have been established by this means throughout the world, and these places act as magnets, attracting others in later generations to the same sites. Places like Stonehenge or Avebury from megalithic times, and more recently cathedrals, mosques, synagogues and temples, are all places that have an accumulation of subtle energy, based on the use to which the space has been put over preceding years. As has already been mentioned, these energies are somewhat akin to radioactive particles in that their intensity diminishes only very slowly. This is why we can still experience the subtle energies from past times, like those that can be found in the temples of Ancient Egypt.

Recognising a power centre

Power centres abound in all sorts of different locations. If you can imagine the amount of spiritual seeking that has taken place over millennia, then you will have an idea of the scope that exists. Obvious choices to consider are places where religious activity has taken place, such as 'holy wells', stone circles, sacred mounds, ancient chapels, temple sites, and so on. However, through analysing the geometric relationship of sacred sites in particular areas I have discovered very powerful centres located in the middle of fields. Power centre sites originating in the megalithic era, in Britain, Ireland and France at least, were not established in isolation but formed groups of centres all energetically linked together through subtle energy channels. By studying the interconnections between such places, through linking them up on a map, it is possible to discover the site of power centres that are no longer obvious today.

Sending energy across space

Subtle energy is not just held locally but can be transferred across space. If you think about the packets of energy flowing out of you all the time, you can actually direct them in a more focused way to another place or person. Indeed, whenever we think of someone a form of connection is made, which is why telepathy works. In effect you project a tiny stream of subtle energy to that person, which creates a bridge allowing thoughts to travel between you.

Let us return for a moment to your imaginary meditation group and suppose that one of your group finds that they have to be away on business for several months, but agrees to 'tune in' with you when you are meeting. Although they are not present physically their mental link will still be effective, enabling them to access and contribute to the quality of the energy you are generating. So effectively their absence should make very little difference to the depth of your meditations or healing work. Indeed, wherever you are, each of you has the ability to access the power you have created between you whenever you want. It is a bit like putting money into a bank; it is there for all of you to draw upon whenever you need it.

Accessing the energy of a power centre

Strange as it may seem, by meditating together in a special room you have in effect created your own power centre, and this is the first step in beginning to learn how to access the energy from more long-standing energy centres. The power from some of these centres can be extremely potent and has the potential to be used for all sorts of Earth healing purposes. However, because of this potency, the power of such places needs to be accessed with a considerable degree of caution. It should be appreciated that there is a big difference between visiting a site in order to tune into its energy, as described above in the discussion on sacred sites, and learning to channel that energy for healing and spiritual purposes. A simple analogy might be the difference between visiting a famous racehorse to stroke its neck and admire its grace and power and then getting into the saddle and learning to ride it in a steeplechase like the Grand National. The one process might lead to the other, but not necessarily. You will need to be very clear about why you want to access this energy, and to what purpose are you going to direct it.

There are a number of important rules that need to be adhered to:

1. INTENTION: Why do you want to access a power centre? Do you have some specific healing applications in mind, perhaps to help heal some of the traumas on this planet? Such energy must only be used for the highest selfless purposes.

2. LOCATION: Seek out only those places where you feel a sense of peace and harmony. Do not try to access the energy of a place just because it is well known. Its energies may not be suitable for you.

3. PROTECTION: Ensure that you use the protection exercise given in Chapter 2.

4. ACCESS: There are specific ways to access and channel the energy from a power centre which will be discussed shortly, but remember the analogy of the racehorse. Each step should be fully integrated before you proceed to the next stage.

Going deeper

All subtle energy is neutral in that it can always be used for either good or evil purposes. It is the intention of the user that determines whether it carries a positive or negative influence. The way in which the peoples of the past guaranteed that the subtle energies of power centres would only be used beneficially was by establishing a form of protection which ensured that only those whose intentions were pure could access this power. These protections are still in place in important centres and come in the form of a guardian whose task is to ensure that the energies of such centres are used correctly. The only way to access the energy is to go through the guardian, effectively to get the guardian's permission to use the energy.

Power centre guardians are spiritual beings who have elected to take on and look after the spiritual energy of a specific centre. It must be emphasised that we are not talking about a man standing over the site in a suit of armour wielding a sword, for these protections have been set up on a spiritual level. How these beings portray themselves to you will be dependent upon your understanding and evolution. In my experience I have met human guardians and angelic guardians, as well as mythical guardians such as dragons and griffins.

Whatever form they take you will first need to be able to contact the spiritual protector of the site before you can channel its energies, and this might take some time to achieve. If you cannot connect with the guardian it may be because you or your group are not yet quite ready to access the power level of the centre. Perseverance is important, as is remembering that when you are ready spiritual doors will always be opened to you. It is the simple principle of the master appearing when the pupil is ready.

When you have satisfactorily connected with this presiding spiritual presence you will be given a pass code or a symbolic key, which you can then use to tap into the energy, channelling it through yourself to sending loving thoughts and balance to whatever healing situation is required on the planet. These symbolic keys act in the same way as the PIN codes we use so freely nowadays. They are always personally allocated, allowing you to gain access to the energy of a particular site, which will assuredly give an enormous boost to your healing and spiritual work.

The energy in these centres is immensely powerful and can be used for all sorts of healing and inner development work. You could focus and direct the energy to help rebalance some of the enormous negativity at present manifesting itself in many different countries in the world. The techniques for doing this will be covered in later chapters.

These energies are an enormous resource for transformation and good, helping to heal the prevailing negativity. Each power centre is like a mini-universe with a kaleidoscope of differing yet complementary vibrational 'energies'. To access what a centre of this type has to offer in its entirety can take many years, so do not be too impatient to move on to discover the next centre. Explore what you have opened up fully before considering looking further afield. As mentioned, these centres often occur in groups, and it is possible to harness the 'energies' of a group of centres, which can considerably increase the effectiveness of your healing work.

Accessing the energy

Let us suppose that you have achieved everything outlined above and have decided that you want to use the available energy in your healing and inner development work. The following are the steps to be taken in order to access the spiritual energy of a power centre. (I would again stress the importance of psychically protecting yourself and the group, if you are working with others.)

1. Carry out the Earth Attunement Exercise, linking to the Earth and Sun, and make sure that you put up your protection.

2. Attune to the energy of the site as described in the previous exercise. If you feel any discomfort with the energies, do not proceed. The means of making additional checks will be given in later chapters, but at a very simple level you could simply ask the Sun to show you a set of traffic lights in your mind's eye. If the lights are red, do not proceed; if amber, proceed only with extreme caution; if green, then you are free to go on to the next stage.

3. Assuming that you have been given a green light, then next try to sense the presence of the guardian. Ask it inwardly to make its presence felt. You will need to be open on all levels to sense its presence.

4. When you sense the presence of the guardian, inwardly ask for permission to use the energy of the site for healing purposes, confirming that you will work only from the standpoint of the highest good.

5. If the guardian adjudges you true of heart you will mentally be given a symbol, which will allow you to access the subtle energy of the site. These symbols can take many forms, including standard ones like a cross or a chalice, but the range is infinite, so do not expect the obvious.

6. If you mentally place the symbol in the centre of the site, a stream of energy will be released through you which you can then focus and send to whatever situation needs help on this planet.

7. With practice it is possible to access the energies of these places from a distance.

There is a great responsibility involved in using the energies from such places, for the misuse of energy can cause many problems. If you are able to access these energies, then use them wisely, for good, remembering that there is always a karmic tab to be picked up if you try to use the energy for selfish or, even worse, malefic ends. It will always rebound on you.

To access the energy from a distance you will need to project your mind to the site and carry out the process outlined above. Once given, the access code can always be used again, so you will not need to get another symbol from the guardian. However, I would always urge people to work as a minimum in pairs if trying to access a site from a distance. One person should keep up the protection around the person who is tuning into the site until all the connections have been made and the energy is flowing. You can then change roles.

If, as in the imaginary example given above, you are part of a group that chooses to mentally access a power centre from a specific place, such as a meditation room, the connection will start to create a tangible energy link that can be detected by others. This is one of the origins of 'ley lines', which will be discussed in greater detail in Chapter 10.

Relocating power centre energy

There is one aspect of energy transference that has been used in the past in relation to sacred sites which is as relevant today as it was then. Let us return for a moment to the imaginary meditation group and suppose that your friend needs to move house but intends to stay in the locality. They have a room in the new property that would be available and suitable for your meditation and healing work. Let us suppose also that by this time you and the group have spent several years building up a strong atmosphere in the meditation room in the old house. Do you have to abandon it and start all over again?

There are two problems that confront you, for not only is it a waste of effort to spend time generating an atmosphere only to leave it behind, but also the new occupants of the house might feel very disturbed by the energy in the room. One man's meat is another man's poison. Strong energies of this type do not suit all people and may actually cause problems for the new occupants – for example, disturbed sleep patterns and suchlike – especially if they have young children.

Dealing with this problem is easy, for you can transfer the energy and re-establish it in the room in the new house. Take the following steps:

1. Carry out all your usual connecting meditations as described in Chapter 1 and then mentally attune to the energy of your room. To make this easier you could imagine that the energy has a colour, such as gold, pink or blue.

2. Next imagine that all the energy and atmosphere are being drawn into an imaginary 'golden chalice' placed in the centre of the room, rather like a genie being drawn back into a lamp.

3. Having drained the existing atmosphere, you need to put something back, bearing in mind the axiom 'nature abhors a vacuum'. Replace the energy that you have withdrawn with something with a more

neutral quality, perhaps by placing an imaginary white rose (a symbol of peace) or something similar in the centre of the room. Visualise this energy filling the entire space.

4. You will now need to project the imagined chalice into the new room, so that when you next come together in the new house you can open it up, allowing all the previously established energy to re-emerge and fill your new meditation space. Before opening up this energy I would first space-clear the room, using the method given in Chapter 7.

Here we see another way in which power centres and sacred sites have been generated, for in this case 'subtle energy' has been moved from one place and located in another. In times past a great deal of energy was moved in this way, and there are a number of power centres in Britain and Europe that had their point of origin in locations other than where they are now.

Finally, if you are part of a long-standing group that decides to disband, then you can always gather up all the energy you have accumulated in the way indicated above and offer it to the Earth to be used in whatever way the spiritual forces of this planet deem suitable.

Chapter 4

Earth Grids, Chakras and Landscape Patterning

Like us, the Earth has a spectrum of interweaving energies, ranging from the physical level to its spiritual dimensions. In this chapter we will explore some of the intermediate realms and energy fields that make up its subtle body, examining how these affect us and in what way we can interact with them creatively.

Physicality and non-physicality

As stated in the previous chapters, energy operates across many spectra. Those energies that belong to the physical world are part of the electromagnetic spectrum, while those that are non-physical I have called subtle energies. We can therefore say that:

1. Physical energies are part of the electromagnetic spectrum and are bound by the normal laws of physics. These energies are held in time and space. Only at the quantum level, at the boundary between physicality and non-physicality, do anomalies occur.

2. Subtle energies are not part of the electromagnetic spectrum and are not bound by the laws of physics,

although some parallels remain. These energies are not constrained by time or space and therefore operate outside the space–time continuum.

Because of the principles of resonance – energy flowing across octaves – there is an exchange between physical energies and non-physical energies. Leading-edge scientists like Professor Fritz-Albert Popp are working on the concept that the bridge between these fields, between physicality and non-physicality, can be found at the quantum level, and that photons of light provide the vehicle for different forms of communication.[‡]

Relevant energies that form part of the physical world include gravitational and magnetic fields, underground streams, microwaves and electromagnetic energies. Energies that are part of the subtle dimension include ley lines, Earth chakras, Hartmann grids, Curry grids, Sha lines, Michael and Mary lines and Platonic grids.

In this chapter we will explore a number of expressions of subtle energy, although in some cases they may also operate on a physical level.

Subtle energy lines

Many people have heard of the term ley lines. They are usually described as lines of subtle energy that criss-cross the Earth's surface. These energies are normally discovered by dowsing – that is, by a person using some object, such as a pendulum or metal rods, to pick up the energy of the lines through the medium of their bodies. What is not generally appreciated is that there are many such patterns that are woven into the matrix of the Earth. Some lines of energy, such as the gravitational fields, do belong to the electromagnetic spectrum, but most, like chakras or

---

[‡]McTaggart, Lynne, *The Field: The Quest for the Secret Force of the Universe*, HarperCollins (2001), pp. 39–60.

Platonic grids, lie outside the physical realm. There is often an overlap between these two complementary but differing states. However, those energies that are part of the subtle realm can only be detected by people (or other sentient creatures), whether through their bodies – by dowsing, for example – or by some other means, such as clairvoyant vision. Because of this complete objectivity is very difficult and, as we shall see, can cause problems.

Water divining

A good example of a skill that lies at the boundary between the physical and non-physical worlds is the proven ability of water diviners to detect underground streams and sources of water, often at considerable depths. The question is whether the diviner is detecting the physical aspect of the water or its subtle energy field. The water is giving off vibrational energy across many spectra. The excitation of its atoms and the flow of its movement are certainly physical, while the emanation from its spiritual essence is non-physical. But which of these levels the diviner is detecting, particularly when dealing with water at depths way beyond the range of scientific equipment, cannot as yet be assessed. Moreover, good diviners can often detect water by simply looking at a map.

The fact that divining works is often taken to mean that the energy source has to be physical, but I believe it can just as easily stem from the subtle realms. We detect these fields through our bodies because our inner wiring ranges across a number of octaves, as described in Chapter 2. Is the diviner picking up the non-physical consciousness of the water in a form of telepathic communication, or tapping into some as yet undetectable energy field emanating from its physical presence?

These may seem like academic points, but the question of physicality or non-physicality is a contentious issue when dealing with these topics. Scientists desperately trying to make everything fit into the electromagnetic spectrum find it hard to grasp this non-physical dimension, while psychics seeking academic approval will sometimes suggest that energy lines, such as ley lines, are a form of magnetic energy. They most certainly are not. We need to be very clear that subtle energies are not part of the electromagnetic spectrum and never will be. Scientists will only fully understand these energies when they embrace the non-physical component of life.

For these reasons, and for the sake of simplicity and coherence, in this chapter, when referring to energies, I am talking about those that lie beyond the electromagnetic spectrum. Some of these energies, in the fullness of time, may prove to be forms of radiation. We can now show that some creatures, like turtles, navigate across vast distances using very minute variations in the gravitational fields of the Earth. It was once thought that these fields were too faint ever to be detectable by the physical body, but we now know differently. However, for the present it seems prudent to duck this issue by affirming that ley lines, Hartmann lines, the Michael and Mary lines,[§] the Sha lines of feng shui, lines of geopathic stress and so on are all part of the non-physical component of our planet, are all subtle energies, and will never, in consequence, be detected by existing scientific equipment.

Thought patterns

The next problem we have to face is what is real and what is unreal in the subtle realm. This may seems like a strange question to pose. The strength of science is that

---

[§]The Michael and Mary lines are dowsed lines discovered by Hamish Miller and Paul Broadhurst which run from Cornwall in the west to East Anglia in the east. Information on these lines was published in *The Sun and the Serpent*, Pendragon Press (1989).

researchers can independently test any concept or theory in an objective way – or at least a relatively objective way. Because subtle energy research can only be conducted through the body it is much more subjective, and therefore determined by our thought patterns. In this belief becomes a very important component. There have been many experiments with dowsers being asked to detect ley lines passing across a piece of open ground. They regularly come up with many different lines. Who is to say what is accurate or not?

If I tell a group of my students that I can detect a 'green spirit energy' located in a corner of a room, even if no spirit is present, then because they trust me their beliefs and thoughts will eventually create an energy field as though a 'spirit' were there. Depending upon the intensity of these beliefs, the packets of subtle energy that have been created, other psychic people who then enter the room will also detect this 'spirit'. The belief might become established as though it were a fact and eventually start to take on a life of its own, with other people detecting 'green spirit energies' in different places. At this point it will have an independent reality. It has effectively become real because of the belief with which it has been endowed. Christ said 'Seek and ye shall find', but he could also have added the corollary 'You will find what you seek'!

Those people who are convinced of a truth will always find reasons to support their beliefs, even in the face of overwhelming evidence to the contrary. No wonder science moves warily in these sometimes murky waters. What I am attempting to do through these pages is present the fruits of my exploration in these realms based upon a caucus of knowledge; to convey what I feel to be valid or correct. I am very open to the view that time might show that the beliefs I hold today may prove illusory. What is important is what you believe to be true. If you believe something is true, then on one level it is true.

Planetary chakras

An example of this is the research that I have carried out into the relationship of the chakras to the Earth. Chakra is a Sanskrit word meaning 'wheel'. The concept stems from Vedic tradition, and many spiritual seekers across the world accept the chakras as subtle energy manifestations connected with our physical make-up. They are normally considered to be focal points of spiralling subtle energy across the front of the human body. Chakras are now widely accepted even though, as yet, there is no scientific evidence to back up the concept, in contrast to acupuncture, where confirmatory changes in electrical skin resistance have been detected. It may be that in time science will discover how chakras connect to the body through resonance, but for the moment we will have to wait for more evidence.

In my view chakras are gateways of energy that link one plane of experience to another. They act as focal points for the transmission of subtle energy across the different octaves or spectra, from the finest spiritual vibrations to the physical, as indicated in Figure 1 (see p. 24). Traditionally there are seven main chakras, which in Western terms are referred to as the crown, brow, throat, heart, solar plexus, sacral and base chakra, depending on their approximate position on the body (see Figure 3 below). Each chakra has a different function – or perhaps more accurately displays a different quality of energy. The heart chakra, for example, acts as a focal point in accessing the energy of love, the brow chakra connects to intuition and new ideas, the base chakra relates to creativity, and so on.

Like the laws of physics, spiritual principles have to be consistent across the whole planet. This is why wars in the name of religion are so senseless. Different spiritual beliefs are simply expressions of how distinct groups

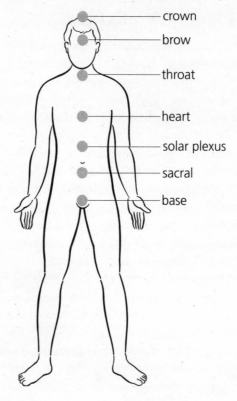

crown
brow
throat
heart
solar plexus
sacral
base

Fig. 3 The chakra positions of the body

perceive these consistent principles. It is rather like taking a famous monument such as the Statue of Liberty and then asking different people to describe what they see as they approach the statue from different directions. Each would perceive the statue from their unique perspective. It is still the same statue, the same Truth, but viewed from a multitude of differing positions, all of them valid. In practice we should welcome these differences because if we could step back a little we could then see an overview from which we might be able to discern the intrinsic essence that is consistent with them all and, in so doing, get closer to understanding the fullness of this Truth.

And so it is with the concept of the chakras. Interestingly, it is just not human beings who have chakras – everything in the natural world does too. Your pet cat and dog have their chakric points, as do your plants, the trees in your garden and, if we extend the concept further, your house, your locality, your country, our world, our solar system, and so on. Each system has its range of chakras and its chakric associations. While the principles are consistent their array of expressions can be different.

In terms of the human frame the chakras are generally shown in a straight line across the front of the body. Even here tradition is not always consistent, with some ancient texts showing different chakras displaced from the vertical axis of the body. But straight-line patterning may be an over-simplification, or only part of the truth. In us chakric energies might be woven around our bodies in bands, as well as being focused at specific places. And if we consider the chakric pattern of the solar system and suggest that each planet represents a chakric energy centre, then, in this case, the focal points are continually moving, as the planets move, in an amazing cosmic dance.

When we come to look at the Earth there are many different approaches we could adopt. For example, do the chakras run from the North to South Pole in a straight line through the centre of the planet, or from the central core to its outer atmosphere? Both are possibilities. Having worked with these ideas for many years and given this matter considerable thought, it seems to me that one obvious level of association is with the continents, in that each continent could be associated with one of the chakras when seen through the lens of their historic and present cultural development.

But before exploring this further, something first needs to be said about the qualities of each chakra. I must emphasise here that I do not see any chakra as being more special or important than any other; each has its own function and quality. The broad associations are as follows:

- **Crown** – connects us to inter-dimensional energies and to those realms of consciousness that lie beyond the physical
- **Brow** – intuition and inspirational ideas, telepathic communication
- **Throat** – communication, intellectual thought, manifestation of ideas
- **Heart** – love, harmony and balance
- **Solar plexus** – emotional drive, vitality and physical energy
- **Sacral** – psychic awareness, receptivity and nurture
- **Base** – creativity, sexual activity, procreation

Chakric associations

Each chakra has a polarity, which allows for the expression of its shadow side. So, for example, the heart chakra also relates to hatred, disharmony and imbalance. The crown chakra carries an energy that allows us to communicate with other dimensions. In an earlier exercise, by linking the light within you through your crown chakra to the Sun, you are, in effect, connecting with the different dimensional energies that emanate from the spiritual aspect of the Sun's energy. The brow chakra is the gateway for new ideas and inspirational concepts. The throat is the main communicator, but also carries a dynamic that allows us to manifest ideas. It makes things happen. The heart allows us to access all qualities of love and harmony, yet at the same time we have to acknowledge its shadow side of hatred and disharmony. The solar plexus chakra provides powerful emotional drives, which can be channelled into organised physical activity but can also give rise to feelings of aggression and fear when not properly balanced. The sacral chakra carries powerful qualities of nurturing. It is what helps sustain the foetus in the mother's womb and also links to the sensitive, receptive sides of our being. In Chinese beliefs it is the Hara point, the place of ultimate balance within the human vehicle. The base chakra activates all aspects of creativity. On a physical level this connects with the sexual drive, but on higher levels provides the dynamic for great works of art and music.

Healing and chakras

When all your chakras are in balance, then you will be in optimum health. In practice there will always be slight imbalances because we are not perfect. But chakric energies can be balanced by healing, and there are many healers today who work solely through the chakras to help balance the energies of their clients. This same principle can be applied to the Earth.

The eighth chakra

As we have seen, traditionally there are seven chakras, but to be progressive I would like to add an eighth. There are a number of reasons for this, but the simplest explanation is that we need eight chakras in order to integrate the concept with the eight primary archetypal qualities reflected in all mythologies and belief systems. An example of this eightfold patterning can be found in the eight directions of feng shui, which is, in effect, another way of looking at chakric energies. I have been studying patterns in many different systems for decades, and an eightfold patterning is much more widespread than those based on the number seven, and has the added advantage of helping us ground energies in the physical.

The chart on p. 268 shows the relationship between many different archetypal principles based upon this eightfold classification. We normally talk of the seven colours of the spectrum, which can be seen when light is projected through a prism, or in the colours of a rainbow. We are, in effect, seeing different wavelengths of the electromagnetic spectrum. However, if we change this linear pattern into a circular pattern, by imagining that each colour forms a segment of a circle, then another colour is created between the red and the violet – the colour magenta. If you take a CD and look at the colours reflected from its surface you will clearly see this magenta colour (which, incidentally, is also one of the primary colours used in colour printing). Perceiving colour in this way was first proposed by the eighteenth-century German philosopher Johann Goethe, and subsequently found its way into Anthroposophy. With the addition of magenta we should therefore really be talking about the eight colours of the spectrum, and not seven. There has been a considerable amount of literature published about the symbolic significance of the octave in music, which again reflects this eightfold symmetry. Seven is a number associated with the circle, which esoterically is always taken as a symbol for the spirit, but an eightfold patterning allows energies to be grounded in the material world. An additional eighth chakra is therefore an important adaptation that reflects the new frequencies of this age.

In fairness, many people have suggested additional chakras, but often these are seen as being above the top of the head. By contrast I would like to suggest that the eighth chakra resides under our feet and holds an energy that links us to the Earth and to our roots or origins on every level. So let us call this chakra the root chakra. As I have stated, it plays a vital role in helping us ground our energies in the Earth and in balancing the energies of the whole system. In this respect we should not forget that Christ washed his disciples' feet and that reflexologists work primarily on the feet, which hold a map of the body, to heal and balance different emotional, physical and mental problems. This would not be possible if the feet were not one of the major chakric centres (see the Appendix for more information on the eighth chakra).

Chakras of the planet

What, then, are the main chakric associations on the planet? I stated previously that we can associate each of the continents with one or other of the chakras. The problem with introducing an eighth chakra is that there are only seven main continents. In practice the area that encircles the North Pole carries an energy that reflects the crown chakra. So, although containing parts of different continents, this area includes countries like Greenland and the northern parts of Finland, Scandinavia, Alaska, Canada and Siberia. The following table gives the planetary chakric areas for the world as a whole, and also splits Europe into its sub-chakras, for this is indeed an infinite process. Each continent has its own set of sub-chakras, often, but not necessarily, focused on an individual country, and each sub-chakra can be further subdivided, and so on. For example, while the British Isles holds the chakric energies of the brow, London carries the throat chakra energies for England.

Chakra	Continent	Europe
Crown	Greenland, Alaska, Artic Circle (taking in a number of continents)	Northern Scandinavian countries, Finland, etc.
Brow	Europe	British Isles, including Eire
Throat	North and Central America	France

Chakra	Continent	Europe
Heart	Asia	Poland, Russia
Solar plexus	Australasia, including New Zealand	Germany, Denmark and Benelux countries
Sacral	South America	Spain and Portugal
Base	Africa	Italy and Switzerland
Root	Antarctica	Greece, Albania and Balkan countries

I have included in the Appendix my chakric suggestions for all the inhabited continents, without in any way wanting to be dogmatic about these associations. Those living in different continents might like to think about how they see these connections for themselves. For example, I would suggest that the Lake Victoria region is the 'heart' of Africa, while Tibet holds the crown chakra energy for Asia, and so on.

By plotting these places on a map you will see that they do not adhere to any straight line as normally associated with chakras on the human body. Straight alignments of chakric energies can exist, as shown in the alignment within Ireland. Yet we can also break down the regions of Ireland into different segments, ascribing a chakric energy to each.

Working with chakric energies

These chakric associations give insight into how patterns or qualities of experience are reflected across the Earth. We can choose to tune into the differing energies of these countries to assess how we relate to them. For example, what is the hidden dynamic of the British Isles that has given this small country – or rather, group of countries – such prominence in the world?

The chakric energies can be focused on your locality,

your particular area of the planet, and also related to any sacred sites that you visit. When visiting such a site, you might like to ask yourself which chakra connects most strongly there and see what happens. Remember that each chakra forms a link from the highest dimensions of spirituality to the physical plane, so do not think that only crown chakra energies are what you should be seeking. The base and the root are every bit as important. Within landscapes in local areas these energies might run in straight lines, although they could also be placed in more complex patterns. Figure 4 gives a chakric alignment that flows through Ireland. This line can be used for healing and balancing the energies of this country, details of which are included in Chapter 7. You can adopt the same principle in your area if you first work out where the chakric energies run.

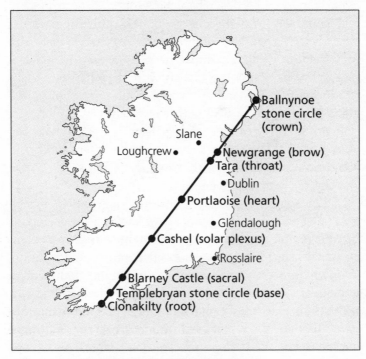

Fig. 4 Chakric line of Ireland

Locating the landscape chakras in your area

Working out where the landscape chakras exist in your area takes time and a willingness to explore your locality. It is not something that can easily be taught because it is dependent upon how you connect with your own chakric system. *The most important principle to appreciate, in beginning this process, is to recognise that there are no right or wrong answers.* This can sometimes be hard to accept, for we are so conditioned into thinking that something is either right or wrong. At one level the chakras can be wherever you want them to be, and this is the best approach to adopt when beginning your search.

I would suggest that you first choose any small area in your locality. This could be a park, a woodland area or even your own garden if you have one. Walk around it, feel your way into the energy of the different parts, as described in Chapter 3, and then try to ascribe a chakra to each section. You can draw these on a map to make it clearer. When you are satisfied with what you have produced, go and stand or sit in the different sections and allow yourself to connect with your own related chakra at that point. For example, if you feel the heart chakra of your garden is located by a rose border, go there and spend some time connecting with your own heart chakra. You can use the exercise given on p. 6 in Chapter 1.

Once you have worked out these patterns in a small area you can expand this concept by looking at the chakras in your region as a whole. I would suggest that you obtain a map of your locality and then spend some time breaking it down into different areas. For example, if there is a woodland area on one side of the map, ask yourself how it feels when compared with a commercial region in another part, for remember that chakric areas can also be found within towns. Visit these places to see what you experience when carrying out the exercise given in Chapter 3, and then try to assess where you would place the different chakras.

Sometimes people like to look for straight alignments and then ascribe chakric energies in the same way that we would within the human body. This is a legitimate approach. Most crown chakra points will be found on the tops of hills, so by looking for the local sacred hill in your area you have a good starting point. You can then see what alignments run from the hill, perhaps passing through other sacred sites or churches, and then make your chakric assessments. By working in this way you might find that some chakras hold very disturbed energies, because of the area through which they pass. This can then offer you an opportunity of working to heal and balance the energy of these places. For example, the heart chakra line of Ireland passes very close to Portlaoise prison, where top-security prisoners are held. This is hardly a good locality for such an important and sensitive place, and indicates that something is amiss with the energies here. By sending healing to this area one is in effect helping to balance the heart chakra of this region, which will in turn help balance the heart chakras of all Irish people.

There is not a nation on this Earth that does not have imbalances, so there is much work that can be done in helping to balance the energies on both a macrocosmic as well as the microcosmic level. Techniques for doing this are given in Chapter 7.

Ida, Pingala and Shusumna

Another model that gives some insight into the energy patterns of the Earth is derived from the Tantric concept of nadis, which are seen as subtle conduits of pranic life-force energy. They carry the life force or spiritual energy to and around our physical bodies. There are thousands of nadis in the body, although only 14 are seen to be of real importance, and three, the Ida, Pingala and Shusumna, of

major significance. The Shusumna, associated with the
spine, links the energy of the base chakra to the crown
chakra in a straight line. The pathways of the Ida and the
Pingala spiral up this central column, crossing at the
chakric centres and bringing a blend of masculine and
feminine energy. If we apply this pattern to the Earth, then
we could imagine that the central axis runs from
Antarctica through Africa and Europe to the Arctic, while
the two flows on either side pick up the Americas on the
one hand and Australasia and Asia on the other (see Figure
5). This concept mirrors the Ancient Egyptian symbolism
of the unification of the two lands, as can be seen in Figure
6, although in this particular case the concept related to
upper and lower Egypt and had only a symbolic association with the Earth.

These patterns give insight into broad areas of energetic exchange, for the Ida carries a more masculine or
active energy while the Pingala is feminine and passive.
The Shusumna represents the point of balance between
these two. From this pattern we can see why certain
regions of the planet, such as Tibet, have held a special or
sacred connection that is relevant to the whole planet
rather that just the region itself.

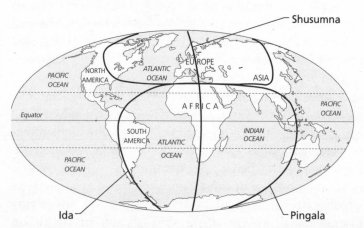

Fig. 5 The Ida and Pingala superimposed on a world map

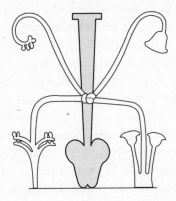

Fig. 6 The union of the two lands – Ancient Egypt

The feng shui connection

Feng Shui has become very popular in recent years. It is the art of balancing subtle energies, known as Ch'i, which make up our environment. It is best known in its application within homes, but it also has wider associations with landscapes and localities. It stems from some of the most profound insights into the nature of subtle energies made in China more than 4,000 years ago. The basic dynamic of all things was considered to be the interweaving of two energies known as *yang* and *yin*. These acted like the two poles in an electrical charge, with yang being all that was positive and outgoing while yin was negative, receptive and inward-moving. These twin energies were further developed into an eightfold patterning known as trigrams, which formed the fundamental basis for the I Ching (the ancient Chinese book of divination) and the eight directions of feng shui known as the Bagua. Each of these trigrams was ascribed a particular quality of energy, and it is the relationship of these eight principles or archetypes which is considered to be the fundamental underlying essence of all things. Feng shui consultants work on establishing a harmony between these principles in their clients' homes or places of work, or in the landscape.

In order to formalise this concept, specific trigrams were ascribed to fixed directions. For example, Kun, the Mother and Earth principle, which also deals with relationships, is associated with the south-west, while the career principle, known as K'an, is connected with the north. This patterning works because of the belief energy that has been invested into it, but it need not be taken as something that is fixed or cast in stone. The principle of finding a balance between the archetypes is absolutely sound, but there are fundamental differences between Chinese and Western thought, so why should the inherent patterning be the same? For example, Chinese design seeks to bring the harmony of nature into the home and garden, while Western thought tries to impose harmonious patterns on the wildness of nature. This comes out in the way we formalise our gardens. Because of these differences straight alignments and long vistas, so prevalent in the West, are anathema in Eastern thought, where more flowing patterns are considered the ideal. In Chinese thought straight alignments give rise to 'Sha' energies, which are always seen as destructive, but alignments linking sacred sites in Britain have exactly the opposite value.

The decision as to how you view these differences is entirely up to you. The concepts embodied in feng shui will work if you believe in them, but you do not have to be bound by this type of prescriptive thinking. Humanity has moved forward 4,000 years, and there are new sets of frequencies that should be considered. There is a correlation between the chakras and the feng shui Bagua, as follows:

Chakra	Trigram	Element	Bagua direction	Chinese quality
Crown	Chien	Heaven	North-west	Helpful people
Brow	Tui	Lake	West	Children
Throat	Li	Light	South	Fame
Heart	Kun	Earth	South-west	Relationships
Solar plexus	Ken	Mountain	North-east	Knowledge
Sacral	Sun	Wind	South-east	Wealth
Base	K'an	Water	North	Career
Root	Chen	Thunder	East	Ancestors

If you are already a feng shui consultant you might like to consider these relationships and then apply them to your work.

One of the great values of feng shui is that it gives us greater insights into the qualities of each of the chakras, and we can apply this when we tune into the chakras of our localities and regions.

We will return later in this chapter to how this information can be used in healing work, but we now need to look at another facet of energy patterning – ley lines – to see how this relates to the chakric energies of different localities.

Ley lines

As already mentioned, ley lines are generally taken to be lines of energy that criss-cross the landscape. The term, in its modern form, comes from the research of a fascinating Victorian gentleman called Alfred Watkins, whose book *The Old Straight Track*** was first published in 1925 when he was already 70 years old. Watkins discovered that many ancient megalithic sites, such as stone circles,

---

**Watkins, Alfred, *The Old Straight Track*, Abacus edition 1974.

long-barrows, tumuli, standing stones and even medieval churches (which he considered were built on much older sacred sites), appeared to be set out in alignments stretching for up to 20 miles. These alignments Watkins called leys because many of the place names through which these alignments passed often ended with the suffix 'ley', as in Casterley. The word ley comes from the Old English word 'lea', which means meadow or forest clearing. Watkins's research focused on Britain, which is particularly rich in archaeological sites dating back to Neolithic times more than 5,000 years ago.

Watkins's leys had nothing to do with energy. They were simply straight trackways, which he believed the megalithic people established as pathways for connecting sacred sites in some form of landscape patterning. It was not until the 1960s that the idea of energy became associated with these alignments. Since then the energy concept has taken off, and those who have heard about leys generally deem them to be lines of energy.

As soon as leys are divorced from the physical alignments proposed by Watkins we hit problems because, as we have stated, dowsers rarely agree between themselves on the alignments. Set a group of psychic people to work on a given area and they will, if not aware of each other's work, invariably pick up very different lines of energy. What might be happening? Is this another of these phantom energies that has no tangible reality? One possible explanation is that these dowsable 'leys' are lines of telepathic energy. In other words when two people set up a conscious telepathic communication between themselves they create a 'ley'. From this it becomes clear that there must be millions of these energy pathways flying backwards and forwards across the planet, for as soon as you think of someone you create a connection to them. They might not be aware of this but the link is made nonetheless. The vast majority of these connections are far too faint to detect but a few are more substantial, rather like the base stations of the mobile phone networks.

Linking energies

In Chapter 3 we mentioned how a group could create an 'energetic' connection between the room in the house where they held their meditations and a sacred site. The more they used this connection the more powerful it would become, so that eventually, like the room in the house, it would start to take on its own unique vibratory quality, which other sensitive people like dowsers could then pick up. From this it becomes apparent that well-known sacred sites might easily have many such connections, depending on how long they have been in use. Moreover, these types of links need not be restricted to sacred sites, for any group that establishes a form of psychic link with another group would create its own ley-line connection. The fact that different individuals pick up different lines is not really a problem as long as they realise what is happening. I would emphasise again here that ley lines have nothing to do with the electromagnetic spectrum. They are subtle energy lines, not physical lines.

If we return to Watkins's ley lines we can see that there is both a factual alignment as well as a potential subtle energy alignment. In my experience the most potent focus of energy is always at the sites being linked. So, for example, in the famous ley that links Stonehenge, Old Sarum, Salisbury Cathedral and Clearbury Ring in Wiltshire, it is these sites which hold the real power, rather than the energy line between them.

Spiritual overview

So why were sites set up in alignment? The origins of site alignment, in Britain at least, go back more than 5,500 years. They were part of the tradition at the time of creating sacred landscapes, which was done by locating different sites, such as standing stones, stone circles and barrows, in a geometric pattern of which alignments are a part. Just as spiritual energy is focused at different locations within us, such as through the chakras, so Neolithic peoples saw the same patterns in the Earth. They established their sites, for religious and spiritual work, in geometrically related groups all linked together energetically. This tradition was taken up in Christian times, and churches were also deliberately set out in alignment together, sometimes oriented to some high point – a sacred hill, for example – for this was the closest point to heaven on a symbolic level.

The way sacred sites are used or why they were set up will influence the connection with one or other of the different chakric energies. Some sites will reflect the full range of chakric qualities; others will be more focused on one or other of the chakric principles.

Landscape circles and patterns

In my book *The Keys to the Temple*[††] I presented evidence for a pair of vast landscape circles that overlie the Marlborough Downs in Wiltshire. I also showed that these circles were deliberately created by a very ingenious people who lived in Britain about 5,000 years ago (see Figure 7). This particular area of England reflects heart chakra energies, and also has an association with the astrological sign of Gemini. And here we have another range of patterns, for astrological influences can also be found woven into the energies of sacred sites.

People who live in the Glastonbury area of Britain are generally aware that there is a large circular landscape pattern overlying this region which reflects the different signs of the zodiac. While there is evidence for this zodiac

---

[††]Furlong, David, *The Keys to the Temple*, Piatkus (1997).

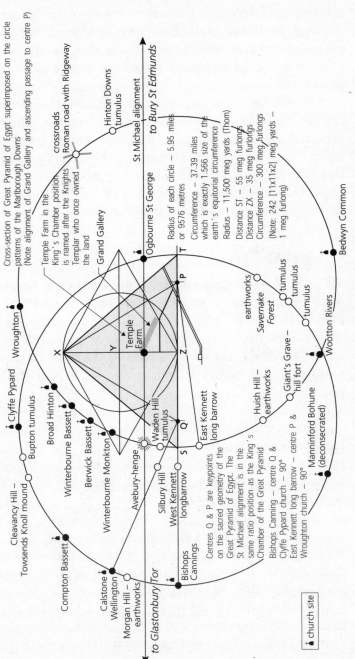

Cross-section of Great Pyramid of Egypt superimposed on the circle patterns of the Marlborough Downs (Note alignment of Grand Gallery and ascending passage to centre P)

Temple Farm in the King's Chamber position is named after the Knights Templar who once owned the land

Radius of each circle – 5.95 miles or 9576 metres

Circumference – 37.39 miles which is exactly 1.566 size of the earth's equitorial circumference
Radius – 11,500 meg yards (Thom)
Distance ST – 55 meg furlongs
Distance ZX – 35 meg furlongs
Circumference – 300 meg furlongs
(Note: 242 [11x11x2] meg yards – 1 meg furlong)

Centres Q & P are keypoints on the sacred geometry of the Great Pyramid of Egypt. The St Michael alignment is in the same ratio position as the King's Chamber of the Great Pyramid
Bishops Canning – centre Q &
Clyffe Pypard church – 90°
East Kennett long barrow – centre P &
Wroughton church – 90°

Fig. 7 The great pyramid pattern of the Marlborough Downs

at a physical level, its primary point of origin is non-physical, for it was established in the far distant past as a portal for spiritual exploration of the qualities held within a twelve-fold celestial pattern – a pattern that we use today as the template of astrology.

This is but one of many such landscape patterns that can be found in the UK and in other countries. I have included a few examples here, but it would be impossible in the space available to do justice to the many patterns that have been set out in the landscapes of different countries. This is something that needs to be discovered by those who live in the regions in question.

Earth grids

The idea of Earth grids has its origins in Ancient Greece. A grid that is used extensively today can be found in the lines of latitude and longitude, which were first propounded by Erastothenes, who lived from c.275 to c.195 BC. These coordinates have nothing to do with energy but are simply an aid to navigation and global placement.

Plato, on the other hand, suggested through his work on geometric solids that these patterns were woven into the development of the Earth's structure. The Platonic solids are the cube, tetrahedron, octahedron, dodecahedron and the icosahedron, and when superimposed on the globe locate nodal points that are part of the building blocks of the Earth.

This idea was taken up by Ivan Sanderson during the 1960s and 1970s when he considered those places on the Earth where there were frequent reports of disturbed phenomena, like the disappearances in the famous Bermuda triangle area. He analysed vast amounts of data from pilots and mariners and finally came to the conclusion that there were twelve equally spaced points on the globe, which he called 'vile vortices', where time-warping events frequently occurred. It is perhaps no surprise that these points coincided with Plato's icosahedron when superimposed on the planet.

Sanderson's ideas were further developed by three Russian scientists, Nikolai Goncharov, Vyacheslav Morozov and Valery Makarov, who produced a map that combined the icosahedron and the dodecahedron. Additional information and research finally led to a planetary grid system devised in 1983 by American professors Bethe Hagens and William Becker (see Figure 8). This grid does appear to have influenced the positioning of the different continents on the planet, although many of its key points fall in the oceans of the world, so it is hard to determine their energetic significance. The placement of the Great Pyramid of Giza on one of the points in Egypt is significant, but then other places of equal importance, such as Lake Titicaca in Peru, do not coincide with the grid, so it does not explain all sacred sites.

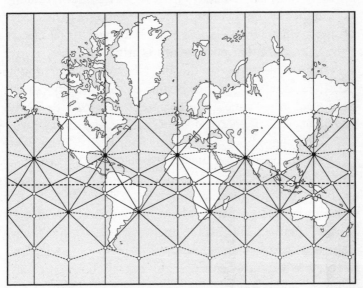

Fig. 8 The Becker-Hagens planetary grid system

Hartmann and other grids

Another grid patterning was discovered by Dr Ernst
Hartmann just after the Second World War. He postulated the existence of a lattice-work of radiations rising
from the ground, each band being about 9 inches or 22
centimetres in width. The grid is magnetically oriented
on a north/south axis, with each band of radiation set
approximately two metres apart, while an east/west grid,
at right angles to the first, runs at 2.5-metre intervals.

Broadly speaking the north/south axis carries yin,
passive or feminine qualities, potentially causing cramps
and rheumatic complaints, while the east/west lattice
reflects a yang, active or masculine, dynamic and is
linked to inflammatory conditions. The spaces in
between are considered a neutral zone, but the crossing
points particularly were thought to be places that could
lead to health problems.

Curry lines, first postulated by Dr Manfred Curry and
Dr Wittmann in the mid-1950s, are very similar in definition to the Hartmann lines. They were thought to be spaced
at approximately three-metre intervals and to be electri-
cally charged, either positive or negative. The pattern gave
a series of responses at the intersections, either double
positives, double negatives or one of each. Curry considered that these lines could potentially lead to health
imbalances when people slept over the intersections.

Although both Hartmann and Curry lines were
claimed to be part of the electromagnetic spectrum no
physical evidence has emerged to support these claims. It
seems to me that they are much more likely to be part of
the subtle energy matrix of the planet. Because of their
nature, neither Hartmann lines nor Curry lines have
gained wide acceptance, although some people who have
worked with these concepts in energy balancing have
achieved some good results.

Physical anomalies

Before we conclude this chapter we need to consider physical anomalies in relationship to sacred sites.

Research is going on at the moment to see whether physical anomalies, such as underground streams or rocks with a high quartz content, are able to induce psychic or spiritual experiences. This is a big subject and the exploration at the moment is in its infancy. We do know that the Neolithic peoples of the past seemed to prefer stones with a high quartz content. Quartz scatters have been found in many stone circles when they have been properly excavated. The façade of Newgrange in Ireland is pure quartz stone and the King's Chamber of the Great Pyramid of Egypt is made of large granite blocks, again with a high quartz content, taken from the Aswan quarries several hundred miles to the south of Giza. The sarsen stones of Stonehenge and Avebury have a high quartz content, and we might wonder why the builders of Stonehenge chose to drag the blue stones all the way from the Preseli Mountains in Wales. Sacred mountains like Stone Mountain near Atlanta in Georgia and Ayers Rock in Australia are also made of granite and sandstone respectively, which enhances their energetic significance.

Scientists like Jacques Beneviste in France have started to discover that water holds memory patterns and can take on the resonance of those substances that have been placed within it, even when so diluted that nothing of the original material remains. This is leading to an understanding of how homoeopathy works. Quartz acts in the same way, for it is possible to project thoughts, concepts or ideas through the mind which then become fixed or held in the crystals.

Many people today are experimenting with precious and semi-precious stones in their healing work with beneficial results, for it has been long recognised that different stones carry slightly different vibrational qualities. Certain shapes and colours can also have an influence, as architects have found in the design of their buildings. These are very slight but do add their contribution to what is sought spiritually by those exploring the subtle energy fields of the Earth.

Healing the landscape

As can be seen from the above, there are many different types of patterning that permeate the Earth, and all can be used for healing. Once you are aware of the type of energy specific to a location then it is quite possible to direct healing energy to the site. What is important is the intention. If you want to help balance a pattern then that intention carries a beneficial thought energy. For example, as already mentioned, in the case of the alignment that runs down through Ireland (see Figure 4) the heart chakra is focused on Portlaoise, which also happens to be the location of the top-security prison. Thoughts of healing and balance can be sent to this area to help the proper expression of the heart chakra energies for Ireland.

It is also significant that the crown chakra, at Ballynoe on the Lecale peninsula by Dumdrum Bay, is not only separated by a stretch of sea from the brow chakra at Newgrange but also by the border between Northern Ireland and the Republic. Whatever happens politically it is still very important for there to be a balanced flow of energies through this entire system, so sending thoughts to facilitate this flow is necessary.

Further details on how we can all send positive thoughts to the planet are given in Chapter 7. In principle we should start with ourselves, by balancing our own energies, and then move on to balance the energies of our homes, before looking to balance those of our locality or country.

Chapter 5

Plants, Trees and Animals

In the last chapter we explored some of the expressions of subtle energy in the world. In this chapter we will look at how it operates within different species and how we can begin to learn to communicate more directly with the plants, trees and animals that coexist with us on this planet. We will consider these species and the place they have in the scheme of life. We will explore how we can work with their healing energies, and in this we should not forget that life is based on exchanges of energy, for it is important to give as well as to receive.

Spirit evolution

Before embarking on an exploration of these different spiritual expressions, I need to offer suggestions as to how all spirit life evolves.

We should begin first by defining the two words *spirit* and *soul*, which are often used very loosely and can cause confusion.

Spirit is the life essence within all living things. It is an evolving consciousness, created by God or the Divine Intelligence, which undergoes a series of experiences before finally returning to the Creator. These experiences can involve a number of physical lives before moving on to the different dimensions of the spiritual planes. This principle applies to all living species, so your pet cat or dog could also have had a number of previous lives, just as you have.

Soul is that part of the spirit directly linked with the body, giving it its life, while the 'higher self' is that part of the spirit which undergoes experience outside the body. We might therefore imagine the spirit as having two halves – the soul, whose primary task is to control and undergo experience through the physical body, and the 'higher self', which can be in touch with other spiritual dimensions.

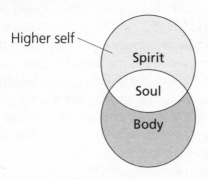

Higher self

Spirit

Soul

Body

Fig. 9 Spirit, soul and higher self

As you can see, there can be overlaps between the terms soul and spirit, but to avoid any confusion in this chapter I will use only the word *spirit*, which I take to mean a point of consciousness or life essence, with its own independent existence, originally created by God.

The birth of a spirit

All spirits are created by God. Spirits manifest themselves both through the life forms that we see on this planet, such as plants, insects, animals and ourselves, as well as through spiritual essences, such as angels, which do not have physical bodies. Each spirit has one supreme gift – that of absolute free will. In this sense there is nothing in the universe that is pre-destined. What happens to each of us throughout our lives is the result of our free-will choices made either while in a physical body or more generally before we entered incarnation in this life. It is your life and it is you who sets the pattern on how it will unfold and is progressing, for better or worse.

The first choice a spirit has to make is to decide which particular route it wishes to take on its journey back to God. Every person who reads this book will have chosen to experience existence through *Homo sapiens* or our evolutionary predecessors, but your spirit could equally have chosen to experience existence through an aspect of the plant, animal or even mineral kingdom. Once the choice is made, however, you are then restricted to that choice. It is rather like getting on an airliner; once on you cannot get off again until the plane lands.

Some schools of thought suggest that we first experience existence through all these humbler life forms before finally becoming human beings. This is not my experience, and I would contend that each stream of evolution – dogs, cats, trees, plants, human beings, and so on – is separate unto itself. This has certainly been my experience when communicating with them.

In the case of human evolution, we go through a number of lives before reaching a stage where we no longer need to incarnate. Some beliefs suggest that this requires many thousands of lives; others that it can be done in one or two. Because we have the gift of free will there are no fixed laws in this context; each spirit must decide for itself, but each spirit also needs to go through a series of filters to reach the next level. It is a bit like sitting an exam – when you have passed you can proceed to the next stage. Metaphorically a spirit can stay for as long as it likes playing in the kindergarten before deciding when it wants to move on to the infants' class, but to make this step it will need to have understood and integrated certain basic principles within its beingness. Seen another way, a moment will come when it no longer needs physical incarnation, and then it evolves solely on the spirit planes.

All life that we see around us goes through the same process. The tree in your garden will experience a number of lives through different species of tree before recognising that it no longer needs to incarnate, and then it will begin its journey initially through the lower spiritual realms before reaching the plane of pure spirit. There is a continual progression into finer and finer dimensions until a spirit finally achieves complete balance and makes that step of merging with God.

The importance of love

It is predominantly through love that we grow in understanding. In order to reach the God level of consciousness we need to understand all experience. This does not mean that we have to directly experience everything, but we have to appreciate everything, which can only be done through assimilating other spirits' experiences. This principle can best be understood through the analogy of computer technology. In order to access another person's experiences, their database, I need metaphorically to network my computer with theirs. When the connection is made I can download my database of experiences into their computer and vice versa. As long as I have sufficient computer capacity I have an infinite number of potential connections or networks that I can make.

On a spiritual level the way this is achieved is through love. When I truly love someone or something, and open my heart to them, then it is possible to begin this downloading process. It requires complete openness and surrender, which are very difficult to achieve while in a physical body, because the ego so easily gets in the way. Generally the achievement is made in the realms of spirit, but we can begin to glimpse the process here on Earth. Your pet cat or dog, if you love them sufficiently deeply, can provide you with an opportunity to begin the process of understanding fully what it is to be a cat or a dog, based on all their physical and spiritual experiences. Individuals who feel an incredible affinity with one or other animal species, or even think they have experienced a life as an animal, will have started to go through this process.

Respect for other species

We need to be able to respect all creatures. This is not to say that some animals are not prepared to give up their lives and be eaten, for this, in some groups of animals, is what they have chosen to experience. However, it is a far cry from keeping an animal in natural surroundings and then humanely taking its life to subjecting it to the unnatural strictures of intensive farming methods. Because of the inter-connection of all life, when we impose suffering on other creatures we are, in effect, imposing it upon ourselves. That suffering can come out in a multitude of different ways, but predominantly it manifests itself through disease.

We now can look at how these principles are reflected in nature.

Trees and plants

Trees and plants go through a similar process of evolution to ourselves, for there is a spiritual consciousness within these species which is evolving just as ours is. On a physical level the plant kingdoms play a vital role in the ecological balance of the Earth, particularly in the maintenance of the levels of carbon dioxide and oxygen. The majority of land-based species are also dependent upon them for food, either directly or indirectly. It is perhaps only those who live in the frozen wastelands in the Arctic regions who rarely come into contact with plants; for most of the rest of us they are a vital part of our lives.

Plants

Plants have both a physical body and a spiritual essence, just as you do. Each has its unique characteristics, so that even two flowers from the same species, such as two daisies in your lawn or even two cuttings from the same plant, will have their own particular vibrational qualities, however slight the differences, because the inner spiritual essence in each is distinct. Those people with 'green fingers' are generally very sensitive to these differences, and are aware of how individual each plant can be. On a physical level plants also acquire a vibrational quality from the particular environment in which they grow.

Plant spirits start their spiritual evolutionary cycle by incarnating into the simpler plant species, such as moss or ferns, before evolving to embrace more complex plant forms, such as those of orchids. They generally enjoy human company and can learn much from us when we tend and cultivate them. They respond to us emotionally but do need respect, which sadly is often lacking in the more intensive farming methods. In return they can give us a sense of emotional and mental ease which human life often militates against.

It was surely no accident which inspired the Buddha to choose a flower – the lotus – as a symbol for meditation, but rather a profound insight into the nature of plants. Nor should we forget Christ's comment about considering the lilies of the field to be more resplendent than Solomon in all his glory. There are many homoeopathic remedies and flower essences in use today that derive their healing power from plants.

Flower remedies

In recent times there has been a proliferation in the use of flower essences for emotional healing purposes. This system was started by Dr Edward Bach in the UK in the 1930s, and has now spread to the rest of the world. It shows the wonderful healing qualities of plants, and how they can help in many different ways.

To gain the greatest benefit from these remedies the producers should ideally communicate with the spiritual consciousness of the plants they are working with, for in so doing they will gain extra help and support in the production of the remedies.

Making flower essences

The original method for the production of the Bach Flower Remedies involved placing plant petals in water and standing them in morning sunlight for several hours. There are producers today who simply place water in a bowl in front of a plant and, communicating with its spirit, ask for its essence to be transmitted into the water. As strange as this may seem, from a scientific perspective it does work, for these remedies have been tested by other sensitive people who have vouched for their efficacy.

Shamans also often use plants in their magical work, employing particular plant substances to induce trance-like states. We should remember the principle that whatever we take into our physical body creates a resonance within that touches our spirit. Learning to know and eat the foods that are right for you is an important part of spiritual growth.

Plant communication

As has now been demonstrated in the laboratory, plants are able to communicate between themselves, through chemical reactions, which is what they do continuously in nature. These systems are usually set up as defence mechanisms against predators, alerting nearby plants of potential threats and even summoning help by attracting other predators to kill off those attacking the plant.[‡‡] If we could but hear on another level we would be aware of a constant chatter going on among the daisies, dandelions and other flowers in our gardens. It is a bit like listening to different pieces of music, which reflect many diverse nuances of feeling. It is not difficult to communicate with plants if you can develop a sensitivity to their moods. They will convey to you whether they are happy or not and when they are stressed through lack of water or misplacement in your room. You will not necessarily hear these communications as words but rather as feelings and an awareness that has no logic attached to it. In return the plants, even in their cut form, will bring you feelings of peace and well-being, which are so valuable in our daily lives. Their spirits for the most part are highly evolved and can put us in touch with those divine qualities which reside within us all. This is why research has shown that a bouquet of flowers is more appreciated by most women than any other single gift.

Plant informers

A close friend of mine is so in touch with her plants that they communicate with her regularly about what takes place in her flat when she is away. On one

---

[‡‡]Max Planck Institute for Chemical Ecology in Jena, Germany (wild tobacco plant studies).

occasion the person looking after her plants while my friend was abroad on a two-week business trip allowed two men to stay over for a couple of nights without permission. When my friend returned the plants told her who had been there and even created a mental image of the two men. When confronted with what she had done the person looking after the plants admitted that it was true. She never found out how my friend discovered what she had done.

Because plants do not have a nervous system, their internal wiring, or the part that allows communication between the spirit and its physical form, is very different from yours and mine. There is no sense of fear of death as you and I know it, and therefore they do not mind being eaten. They do not experience pain through their physical bodies in a direct sense, but can be upset by thoughts and attitudes towards them.

Plant Attunement Exercise

Aim: To begin the process of learning to communicate with a plant

Time: 10–15 minutes

Choose a potted plant or a plant in your garden with which you feel an affinity. Spend some time sitting with the plant, sensing the qualities that make it special to you. Sit in the position for meditation given in Chapter 1.

1. Imagine that you are shrinking in size to the same height as your plant and are then standing next to it. Observe your feelings. How does it make you feel?

2. Imagine that you are touching its leaves and flowers. What sensations do you experience? Then imagine that you are standing within the plant, feeling its power and essence. Connect to your heart and send the plant your love and gratitude for what it provides.

3. Now slowly imagine that you are blending with the plant so that you become it and it becomes you. What does it feel like to be this plant? What do you now experience?

4. Now sense the quality that this plant brings into your house or garden and how it communicates with other plants around it.

5. When you have experienced this fully, slowly disconnect from the plant so that you feel separate from it once more, and in your imagination return to your normal size and position next to it.

6. Now try to communicate with the plant while in this state, asking it questions in your mind and seeing whether you can sense any information that it wishes to convey to you. This might come in the form of words, picture images or simply feelings. Although this may be difficult at the beginning, try to hold this connection for several minutes.

7. Finally thank it for its help and bring yourself back to full waking consciousness.

It is natural when gardening to remove those plants that one does not want, including what we loosely describe as weeds. This is an accepted part of the life pattern of plants, which recognise that part of their role is to act as food for other species, so they are not averse to being pulled up, removed and digested. When weeding or digging up plants, tell them first in your mind what you are going to do and why you are going to do it and they will not be affronted.

Those who tend and nurture plants are opening themselves to a wonderful form of energetic exchange. Through our free will we can enhance the beauty of nature, although nature is incredibly beautiful without human interference. Yet the bringing together of plant species from different parts of the world allows them to experience a greater diversity of communication. Send love to your plants, and bless them when you plant them in the soil, and they will repay you a thousand-fold.

Plant associations

There is a vast range of plant associations with different psychological and emotional states. A full book could be written on this subject alone. A brief list to whet the appetite is included here. Some of these attributes are based on the flower remedies; others stem from traditional folklore associations.

Flower associations

Agrimony	Overcoming mental torment
Bluebell	Opens the heart, joy
Century	Strength of mind and character
Cerato	Strength in decision-making
Clematis	Connection to other worlds
Daisy	Innocence and grace
Dandelion	Light-heartedness and fun
Dog rose	Confidence, courage
Fuchsia	Letting go of negative thoughts
Gentian	Joy and uplifting of mood
Heather	Connection to others

Honeysuckle	Being present with self
Impatiens	Patience
Iris	Spiritual insights and awakening; light, hope and letting go of sorrow
Lily of the valley	Humility and spiritual love
Lotus	Inner peace
Marigold	Openness of heart and fidelity
Mimulus	Overcoming known fears
Orchid	Spiritual aspiration and beauty
Peony	Good fortune, riches and glory
Rose	Protection and love
Sage	Cleansing and protection
Scleranthus	Decisiveness
Star of Bethlehem	Overcoming shock
Tulip	Symbol of perfect love
Water violet	Overcoming shyness
Wild violet	Letting go of worry and fear
Wisteria	Gentleness
Yarrow	Protection and divination

Trees

Trees are sometimes regarded as the monarchs of the plant kingdom, although in reality they form a distinct spiritual species. Plants, in their evolutionary cycle, do not progress into incarnating into trees; neither does a tree spirit incarnate into a flower such as a hollyhock. Each adheres to its own grouping. Tree spirits have been given a variety of names, in different cultures, but the term dryad, used by the Ancient Greeks, suits them well and is the most widely adopted term today. Like plants trees communicate between themselves both through their roots and through their leaves. Apart from helping with oxygen balance, their primary role on the planet is the drawing down of 'higher' vibrational energies from the Sun and other cosmic bodies and fixing these energies in the Earth. They are great conductors and transmitters on every level.

The spiritual role of trees

Most animal species on the planet have their primary orientation, their 'backbone', horizontal to the plane of the Earth. These species are involved with weaving a web of subtle energy around the Earth. Plant species, through their petals and roots, predominantly act in the same way. However, trees, like human beings, have a strong vertical axis, which, like a lightning conductor, allow spiritual energies from the cosmos to be channelled through to the Earth. We too have a role to play in drawing down spiritual energies and focusing them on the planet, as you experienced in the Earth Connection Exercise in Chapter 1. This is one of the reasons why trees have played such a significant part in human mythology. The Earth requires a wide range of frequencies in its evolutionary patterning, and the orientation or backbone of a species gives clues as to its energetic role. This is why, when meditating, people are encouraged to keep a straight back, as this facilitates the flow of energy from the cosmos to the Earth.

Trees have been around on this planet for more than 360 million years, which means we are relative babes to them in evolutionary terms. Their longevity, from hundreds to even thousands of years, also gives them an advantage in awareness, so we should bear in mind that there is much that they can teach us. The Buddha gained his enlightenment under a tree and Odin discovered the runes while hanging in the Yggdrasil, the Scandinavian 'Tree of Life'. Nor should we forget that it was the Tree of Knowledge of Good and Evil which opened our eyes and set us forth on our journey from the Garden of Eden.

The language of trees

In my own experience trees have generally communicated to me verbally – that is, I can hear the words they speak in my head. I sometimes speculate on whether this is my own psyche translating their messages or whether it is a linguistic ability that trees possess. For many years I wondered whether my tree communications were just a result of my own lively imagination, until one day a particularly chatty Atlantic cedar gave me some factual information about a friend that I was then able to verify. Since then I have not doubted their messages.

An Atlantic cedar communicates

This particular tree stood in a beautiful garden, and I would often stop by for a chat with it, admiring its beautiful shape. Like many trees it looked after the balance of subtle energy in the area. One day it told me that it had once given some healing to a friend of mine, for trees are great healers. This gave me some information that I was then able to verify, for this friend did admit that, following the death of her husband, she had spent almost the whole of one day sat under this tree, sobbing her heart out. She felt the tree had helped soothe her inner pain and turmoil.

Trees speak as they find and as they perceive life to be. Some carry a more masculine quality while others are distinctly feminine. They are amazing healers, and like plants have a wonderful ability to soothe hurt minds and distressed emotions. They accept the need for humans to use their wood and generally are very willing to give up their lives in this cause. They are, however, distressed, as is the Earth itself, when vast swathes of forest are cleared indiscriminately. Far better to thin a forest out than to log complete areas. The energetic balance of the planet is disturbed in the latter case, which has repercussions on many different levels. At the moment the climate of the Earth is changing. This is not solely the responsibility of human beings, but we do have to accept our part in the process, caused primarily through deforestation and pollution, which in years to come is going to have some devastating consequences for us.

To communicate with trees you need to spend time with them. Ideally you should seek out a tree that you can visit regularly, a tree that can become a close friend. This may take a little time but the rewards when you achieve it are immense, for trees can help us find much-needed balance and integration in our lives. As in the case referred to above, they are wonderful at helping soothe emotional problems and dispelling clouds of doubt and despondency. They can also help us ground our energies so that we find sorely needed harmony with the Earth itself. Once you have found your tree you will then need to spend time communicating with it along the lines given in the following exercise.

Tree Attunement Exercise
Aim: To begin the process of learning to communicate with a tree
Time: 10–15 minutes

Choose a tree in your garden or neighbourhood with which you feel an affinity. Try to spend some time observing the tree and sensing the qualities that make it special to you. At a suitable time, find a place indoors where you can be quiet and undisturbed. Sit in the position for meditation given in Chapter 1.

1. Imagine that you are standing next to your chosen tree and observe your feelings.

2. Imagine that you are running your hands over its bark. What sensations do you experience? Then imagine that you are standing with your back to the tree, feeling its power and solidity pressing against your back. Connect to your heart and send the tree your love and gratitude for what it provides.

3. Now slowly imagine that you are blending yourself with the tree so that you become it and it becomes you. What does it feel like to be a tree? What do you now experience?

4. Now sense that as a tree your imaginary roots are connecting you deep into the soil, helping you feel really connected to the Earth. What does this feel like?

5. Next slowly disconnect from the tree so that you feel separate from it once more.

6. Try to communicate with the tree while in this state, asking it questions in your mind and seeing whether you can sense any information that it wishes to convey to you. This might come in the form of words, picture images or simply feelings. Although this may be difficult at the beginning, try to hold this connection for several minutes.

7. Finally thank the tree for its help and bring your-self back to full waking consciousness.

It is often easier to carry out this exercise in the comfort of your own home than on-site, where you might feel very self-conscious. However, with practice it becomes possible to connect to a tree very quickly using this method, so that you will be able to try it out on trees there and then. A few minutes' quiet communication with a tree that catches your awareness can prove very rewarding. They all have their distinct 'personalities', and some are much more communicative than others. You will also find that trees enjoy rest periods – and not just in winter – when they cannot easily be contacted.

Magic wands

Although each tree has its incarnate dryad spirit, other tree spirits will often permeate the tree, creating a group of tree spirits. These individual tree spirits can sometimes be persuaded to enter a cut stick, staff or wand and remain connected to it. Magic wands infused in this way allow an individual to maintain a more direct communication with this type of spirit. If you can achieve this they will assist you in your healing work, either with people or with different aspects of Earth energy work.

Depending on what you have in mind you will need to select your wood from a living tree. To do this you will first need the permission of the owner of the tree (most trees have human owners) and then also ask for the cooperation of the tree spirit, telling it fully the purposes to which you want to put the piece of wood.

There are many different types of trees to choose from, and a list of their attributes is given below. The procedures I would adopt are as follows:

1. To cut the tree I would wait until around midday, when its vitality is at its greatest, although some people prefer to cut their selected branch in accordance with the phases of the Moon.

2. Tell the tree what you are going to do by sending it a mental message or image. Wait for its response and only proceed if you get a positive answer. If you are not sure how to do this then use the traffic light metaphor given in Chapter 3. Only proceed if the light turns green.

3. Cut the piece to the length you require, depending on whether it is for a small wand or a staff. At the moment of cutting the energy or 'life force' of the dryad normally leaves the detached piece.

4. To reverse this process, once it is cut place the detached piece next to the tree and leave it there overnight, telling the tree that you would like a dryad spirit to enter the wood so that you can work cooperatively with it, perhaps for healing purposes, or something similar.

5. Collect the piece of wood the following day and thank the tree for its help. Provided you have carried out the procedures correctly and the spirit of the tree deems you suitable, your wand, or staff, should now be 'alive' with a new dryad spirit with which you can begin a more direct spiritual connection. This will not be the spirit of the tree but another dryad that is open to working with you.

6. One practical point: do not leave an open wound in the tree for infections to enter. A clean cut and a suitable sealant are appropriate here.

Tree lore

Each tree species has acquired different associations in the many cultures of this world. The correspondences given below are but a small contribution based on an international list. Each tree is unique, but there are similarities within a species just as there are cultural affinities within the different tribes of the Earth. (The astrological signs and the planetary associations for these trees do not conform exactly with standard astrological concepts but have been derived from inner guidance.)

Alder – associated with fire and the Celtic god Bran. It also has connections with King Arthur. The alder is the tree of the warrior, representing steadfastness to inner principles. Astrological sign: Aries. Planet: Mars.

Apple – the tree of love, fertility, joyousness, knowledge and poetic inspiration. The apple is the fruit of Aphrodite, the Greek goddess of love, and in ancient China was the symbol of peace and beauty. The gardens of paradise, the Hesperides, were filled with apple trees tended by nine fair maidens who were part of the retinue of Aphrodite. It is the Tree of Knowledge in the Garden of Eden and the eating of its fruit led to a new state of awareness for Adam and Eve. The tree is said to bestow great healing benefits; various elements have been used for creating love potions and in the Bach remedies crab apple is used for cleansing and purification. Astrological sign: Libra. Planet: Venus.

Ash – the cosmic tree, the 'Yggdrasil', from which all life sprang, according to the Teutonic and Scandinavian peoples. Odin hung for nine days on this tree and afterwards was given the runes, the magical signs associated with the alphabet, which were also used for magic and divination. Because of the straightness and pliability of its wood it is very suitable for making weapons, particularly spears and staves, so that it became the favourite and magical tree of the warrior. In this context it also became associated with rebirth and new life, the right of any warrior who died gloriously in battle. The tree is also associated with the Sun and carries strong solar healing energies. Astrological sign: Aquarius. Planet: Uranus.

Aspen – from the same family as the poplar, the aspen has a distinct place in Celtic tradition. Its wood was used by Celtic warriors to make magic shields against all forms of adversity, and its trembling leaves were used for divinatory purposes by the Druids. It helps us face our fears, according to the Bach remedies, and to confront the negative or shadow aspects of our being. Astrological sign: Sagittarius. Planet: Neptune.

Beech – the tree of prosperity and good cheer. According to the Bach remedies, it helps us to discover the positive things in life, to see our glass as half full rather than half empty. It is sometimes seen as the mother of the woods because of its protective, nurturing nature, and its edible nuts. It is the queen which stands beside the oak king. It is also thought that the first words of instruction were written on beech bark, for it is from the Anglo-Saxon word 'bok', meaning beech, that we derive our present word 'book'. This association links the tree to all forms of ancient wisdom and the accessing of the past through meditation and inner attunement. Astrological sign: Virgo. Planet: Earth.

Birch – associated with the Celtic goddess Brigid, who has three distinct roles as warrioress, poet and mother. It was claimed to have the power to 'drive out the Devil', which is the origin of the caning of felons and lunatics. The birch was used for many divinatory purposes, as well as the making of runes and magic staves. It is a lucky tree, bringing good fortune to those who work with its energy, and helps to clear out the old to make way for the new. The birch is the 'Cosmic Tree' of shamanism, allowing ascent to the level of the Supreme Spirit. Astrological sign: Virgo. Planet: Mercury.

Cedar – the tree of strength, nobility and incorruptibility. Solomon's temple was built with this tree and the word 'deodar' (one of the species of cedar) literally means 'tree of the gods'. It is the most commonly named tree in the Bible and in Hindu tradition is associated with Shiva, Parva and Vishnu. To the Sumerians it was the 'Tree of Life', possessing sacred properties, and it was also sacred to Tammuz, one of the Sumerian gods. It is also associated with the Egyptian god Osiris. Astrological sign: Cancer. Astronomical body: Sun.

Chestnut – strangely not associated with any of the Celtic traditions. In the Bach remedies the white or horse chestnut helps those with a chattering mind who are continually bombarded with unwanted thoughts, while the red sweet chestnut strengthens those who are driven to the limits of their endurance. Astrological sign: Sagittarius. Planet: Jupiter.

Elder – the tree of change and transition from one state to another which has been associated with witchcraft and magic because of its powerful spirit known as the Elder Mother. Superstition has it that cutting or harming this tree brings bad luck down on the person who does it, unless he or she has first been given permission by this being. The berries and flowers make a wonderful wine, and this connection suggests a link with the ability to see and communicate with the other worlds, for intoxicating drinks, like hallucinogenic substances, have long been associated with shamanic practices. Astrological sign: Cancer. Astronomical body: Moon.

Elm – a tree of purification and cleansing. Tradition also tells that it is the tree of elves, and was especially important for contacting the spirits of the forests. In the Bach remedies elm is used when individuals are under great stress, bringing the fortitude to soldier on. In Christian tradition it represented the power of the scriptures for the faithful. Astrological sign: Capricorn. Planet: Saturn.

Eucalyptus – a native species from Australia that has now found its way to many regions of the world. The oil from the tree has strong soothing properties, particularly for lungs, sinuses and nasal passages, and also helps combat colds, flu and chest infections. Its essence is used to tackle feelings of loneliness and the need to accept life as it is. Astrological sign: Gemini. Planet: Mercury.

Fir – associated with good health and strength, and with transformation, when needed, to a higher or better state with new insights and objectivity. It is one of the Ogham trees[§§] of Celtic mythology, denoting the beginning of things. Astrological sign: Aries. Planet: Mars.

Ginkgo – deeply revered by the Buddhists of China and Korea, and also planted by Shinto priests in their temple areas. It is one of the oldest living species on this planet, dating back more than 200 million years. It falls into neither of the two main categories, broad leafed or conifer, but belongs to its own order (*Ginkgoopsida*), of which it is the only surviving member. Ginkgo leaves have a number of medicinal qualities which are used for treating various conditions such as tinnitus, chilblains, strokes, senile dementia, memory loss and dizziness. Astrological sign: Aries. Planet: Mars.

Hawthorn – its flowers are claimed to be the meeting place of fairies, and were also used in bridal ceremonies in Ancient Roman times. It is therefore one of the prime trees of fertility. Its garlands traditionally adorn the May Queen and hence there is a close connection with the Celtic festival of Beltane. The famous Glastonbury Thorn miraculously sprang from a staff made from the wood of the tree that Joseph of Arimathaea had placed in the ground. This led to an association with Christ and his crown of thorns. Astrological sign: Taurus. Planet: Venus.

Hazel – associated with the Earth Mother goddess, thereby connecting with divination, wisdom, intuition and dowsing, as dowsers' rods have traditionally been made of hazel twigs. In Ancient Greece the wand or caduceus of Hermes, the messenger of the gods, was made of hazel, so

---

[§§]The lore of the trees, or Ogham, became part of a secret language known as Beth-Luis-Nion, in which each letter of the alphabet was ascribed to a tree. There were 24 trees in Ogham, the eight noble trees being birch, alder, willow, oak, rowan, hazel, apple and ash.

it also relates to communication, travel and healing. In Scandinavia it was sacred to Thor, the god of thunder. The salmon of wisdom of the Celts gained his knowledge by swallowing nine hazelnuts. Astrological sign: Gemini. Planet: Mercury.

Holly – a tree of winter, being used in midwinter solstice festivals, and associated with immortality and rebirth. Its prickly leaves have traditionally made it a man's tree, connected with the stories of the Holly King, who salutes the Sun after the longest winter day. In this context Christ is also seen to be embodied in the holly, its red berries representing His blood. In the Bach remedies holly is used to treat over-sensitivity, hatred, anger and aggressive behaviour. Its essences can also be used for protection against negative influences. Astrological sign: Capricorn. Planet: Saturn.

Ivy – the feminine ivy needs to cling to others for support but being evergreen also stands for immortality and eternal life. It is connected to the Greek god Dionysus, and it is claimed that the ivy helps diminish drunkenness. This tree also symbolises friendship, faithfulness and constancy even in the face of adversity. The Christmas carol 'The Holly and the Ivy' symbolises the dance between the masculine and the feminine. Astrological sign: Cancer. Astronomical body: Moon.

Lime – also known as the linden, this tree expresses feminine grace, beauty, happiness and, above all, love. In European folklore the linden was sacred to Freya, the Teutonic goddess of love and fertility. In medieval times lime blossoms were used as a symbol of romantic love. In Greek mythology Philyra, the mother of the centaur Chiron, turned herself into a lime tree. In Scandinavian mythology the lime was said to be the haunt of elves and fairies, and it was considered dangerous to be near one of these trees after dark. Astrological sign: Libra. Planet: Venus.

Oak – sometimes called the monarch of the forest because it was sacred to both Zeus/Jupiter, the king of the Greco-Roman gods, and to Dagda, the supreme god of the Celts. The oak brings strength, durability, protection and courage. According to Greek tradition it was the tree from which all humanity sprang, and the oak forest of Dodona, sacred to Zeus, became one of the primary oracle centres of the ancient world. It was the most important magical tree of the Druids, particularly when covered with mistletoe, and the term 'druid' possibly comes from the Gaelic word 'duir', which means oak. In the Bach remedies it helps people fighting against great difficulties. In the Amerindian traditions it is the sacred tree of the Earth Mother. Astrological sign: Leo. Astronomical body: Sun.

Olive – the tree of peace, hope and friendship. It has played an enduring role in the lives of the Mediterranean peoples, providing them with both fruit and highly prized oil. To the Romans the olive was sacred to Minerva (the Greek Athene), the goddess of health and wisdom and to Muslims it is the 'Tree of Blessing giving to the world the light of Allah'. It was on the 'Mount of Olives' in the garden of Gethsemane that Jesus was seized before his crucifixion. Olive oil has many medicinal properties, and in the Bach remedies its essence is used for those who feel mentally and physically exhausted. It assists in combating the effects of overwork and stress, helping people get through any of life's crises. Astrological sign: Pisces. Planet: Neptune.

Pine – the tree of foresight, vitality, uprightness and purification. Its evergreen leaves bring immortality and its wood was traditionally used to make coffins, being thought to preserve the body from corruption. The pine cone sat atop the wand, the thrysus, of the Greek god of wine, Dionysus, as a symbol of fertility and fecundity. In the Bach remedies pine is used to help those who suffer from reproach and self-blame. It helps clear all negative influences and can be used to ward off malignant forces. Astrological sign: Aquarius. Planet: Uranus.

Poplar – the tree of the balance of polarities between yin and yang, according to Chinese tradition, because of the distinct two-tone effect of the upper and lower sides of its leaves. Hercules used a crown of poplar leaves when he descended into Hades, so it brings protection and help for those who want to access the Plutonian aspects of their nature. Astrological sign: Scorpio. Planet: Pluto.

Redwood – the tallest of all living tree species, reaching, in some cases, a staggering height in excess of 100 metres. These trees were sacred to the Tolawa peoples of the Pacific coasts of Oregon and California, and were regarded as the protectors of the whole forest and the home of the ancestral spirits. Astrological sign: Leo. Planet: Earth.

Rowan – also known as mountain ash, and associated with one of the great Celtic gods, Lugh. His magical weapon was the spear, highlighting his warrior qualities. The rowan tree brings insight and forewarning of events to come, and has a special power for guarding magical places such as stone circles and sacred sites. Sometimes used instead of hazel for divination, it provides protection against enchantments. Astrological sign: Capricorn. Planet: Uranus.

Sycamore – the Ancient Egyptian Tree of Life, being associated with the sky goddess Nut and particularly with the great Mother Goddess Hathor, who was known as the Lady of the Sycamore. Portrayed as a cow, Hathor brings joy, nourishment, fertility and love to all who revere her. The sycamore is also connected with the Greek goddess Artemis, the huntress. Astrological sign: Aquarius. Planet: Uranus.

Vine – because it produces grapes, the source of passion and fertility, liberating the unconscious desires from inhibitions. It helps us access our intuition and inspires us to new states of awareness. It is the tree sacred to the Ancient Egyptian god Osiris, and Christ is sometimes depicted as the true vine and his disciples as the branches bearing the fruit of his teaching. In Greco-Roman tradition it is associated with Dionysus, and hence with the psychic aspects of our nature. In the Bach remedies it is used for those who are over-assertive and more inclined to pay attention to others rather than look within themselves, which is often a defence against dealing with one's own shadow issues. Astrological sign: Pisces. Planet: Neptune.

Walnut – introduced into Britain in Roman times, it lives to a great age. The nuts symbolise hidden wisdom and were served up at wedding feasts in Greek and Roman times. It stands for strength in adversity, and the caryatids are nut nymphs in Greek mythology. In the Bach remedies walnuts are the link-breakers with the past, helping us to let go and move on and providing constancy and protection from outside influences. Astrological sign: Sagittarius. Planet: Jupiter.

Willow – has very close connections with water and was therefore used for water divination. The traditional witch's broom comprised ash for the handle, birch for the broom and willow to bind them together. Willow has several medicinal agents, including salicylic acid, which was used to relieve rheumatic pains. The willow is associated with intuition and psychic activity. Astrological sign: Pisces. Planet: Neptune.

Yew – its association with churchyards, often located on more ancient Druidic sites, gives some clues as to its qualities – its connection with life, death and rebirth. The wood was used for making longbows in the Middle Ages and its superior flexibility makes it an ideal wood, when polished, for magical staves or wands. Astrological sign: Scorpio. Planet: Pluto.

Animal evolution

How often have you had your pet cat or dog gaze into your eyes and wondered what was going through their minds? Animals have souls just like us, and they go through a similar evolutionary spiral on a spiritual level. Broadly speaking, domesticated animals and particularly pets are on a similar level of spiritual evolution to human beings. I have met some animals that housed very evolved souls, and there has been a wonderfully deep communication between us. I equate these with the gurus of the animal world. It is very important that by virtue of human arrogance we do not confuse spiritual evolution with somatic or physical evolution.

Of all the creatures on this planet human beings derive the greatest benefit from the gift of free will. However, this does not make us spiritually superior. Indeed, if we were to apply the criterion that an expression of the level of spiritual evolution of a species is its ability to live in harmony with its environment, and also to assess the degree of our symbiotic relationship with the Earth, then human beings do not fare too well.

As has already been stated, because of the alignment of their backbones animals are much more in tune with the psychic web of subtle energy that flows around the planet. This is why they can pick up the signals of impending earthquakes before scientific equipment. There is much that they could teach us on this level if we would but open up to conducting a dialogue with them. Such levels of communication will not happen overnight, but as more and more people find that they can both send and receive messages from their pets, the more this facility will become available to us. We too are evolving, but for a long time we have neglected our psychic senses and our ability to easily access the information that is available on a subtle level.

Telepathic communication

The brains and nervous systems of mammals and birds are structured like ours and in consequence they have very similar ranges of responses, through their physical senses, to their surroundings. They feel pain as we do. Animals communicate physically through sound, movement and display, but they also can project mental images in a form of telepathic communication. This is how we can begin to communicate with them more directly. As a species, we have allowed our telepathic proficiency to atrophy, which means that it requires quite a lot of practice to master the skill of a two-way communication with your pet cat, dog or budgerigar.

Dogs are often the easiest animals on which to practise sending visual images, although cats generally have a more highly developed telepathic ability than dogs, but being more introverted are generally not so forthcoming in their responses. They do make excellent psychic helpers and will assist individuals engaged in healing activities, acting as protectors and channellers of healing energy. Cats will always adopt a sphinx-like pose when working in this way, so it is quite easy to tell whether your feline friend is assisting you or not.

There have been numerous accounts of the extraordinary ability of animals to track down their owners when they have inadvertently gone astray during a house move. There are also many accounts of dogs in particular knowing instantly when their favoured human is returning from work, even at a distance of several miles and when the timing is irregular. They can be incredibly loyal and offer a non-judgemental love to those whom they see as part of their family. However, they also experience the full range of emotional responses that we ourselves enjoy – or not, as the case may be. They can be very jealous and protective of those whom they see as their family, and can display anger and aggression just as we do.

In her remarkable book *Straight from the Horse's Mouth*, Amelia Kinkade describes her experiences in animal communication and the amazing stories they have to tell. She provides a series of excellent exercises to help develop our telepathic skills, enabling us to open up to the whole gamut of animal communication. Amelia can also 'hear' animals talk in the way I have described with trees, although in my own case communication has always been through projecting and seeing mental images. Here is an extract from her book, which deserves to be quoted in full.

It does not matter whether you teach your dog to sit and shake a paw. What matters is that you learn from her (or him). What can you learn from a dog?

How to really enjoy life. Spontaneity. Endless exuberance. The spirit of adventure. Affection given freely. Compassion. Forgiveness. How to free your heart. Passion. Courage. Trust. Faith. Devotion. How to abolish worry, anxiety, and fear of death. Lack of self-judgement. Lack of self-doubt.

They are here to bring our attention to the here and now. They open our hearts and teach us how to love unconditionally . . .

What can you learn from your cat?

Grace. Power. Fearlessness. Patience. The element of surprise. Carefreeness. Healthy boundaries. Self-protection. Dignity. Risk taking. Trusting your impulses. Aggressiveness. Acting on instinct. Impeccable timing. Speed. Balance. Recovery. How to sleep without worry. How to astrally project and walk between worlds. How to heal. How to return from death. Elegance. Sophistication. Inner peace. High comedy.

Animals are here to teach us how to love. In our society, our thinking is backward. When learning to talk to animals consider this: Why should they talk to you? Why should they listen to you? Your stance in communication must be based on humility ... Make a habit of explaining to animals why you are a human who can talk to them. (Because you love them.) In establishing a foundation of trust, you might try sending some reassuring ideas like this:

Trust-building thought-forms
    I love you
    I won't lie to you
    I won't trick you
    I'm here for you, to help make you happy, to give you whatever you need. If you tell me what you want, I'll do whatever I can to help you get it.
    Believe me when I tell you, your animals will hear you. They will understand. Your animals will comprehend every word you say, but they might not be accustomed to having you listen to them.
    Here are a few lessons in listening:
    Ask for their help
    Ask for their patience
    Take them seriously. Don't patronize.[***]

Projecting images

To communicate with your pet you will need to learn to create picture images in your mind. For example, you can visualise your dog and yourself going for a walk and then imagine that you are placing this picture in the dog's mind. It will very quickly learn and respond to you. Picking up the reply is a bit more difficult and requires an ability to still the mind and allow pictures and feelings to surface simultaneously. You can use the exercise for tree communication but replace the tree with your favourite pet or

[***]Kinkade, Amelia, *Straight from the Horse's Mouth*, Thorsons (2001), pp. 90–1.

animal. It does not have to be one that you own, and these exercises can also be carried out at a distance.

In the tree exercise I suggested that we can experience something of what it is to be a tree by imagining that we have become one. You can adopt the same concept with animals. In imagining you are becoming your pet, try to sense what feelings emerge, for animals do express the same range of emotions as you and I. They can feel joy, sadness, excitement, and so on. I have been privileged to communicate with some highly evolved animals in my time, both cats and dogs, and know that there is much they can teach us. Animals are not as judgemental as human beings, and will add sympathy and emotional balance to your life.

In learning to conduct a dialogue with them you can find out those aspects which make their life more enjoyable and pleasant. You can also relay to them your particular wants and needs. A good dog handler will also project mental pictures to their pet, telling them what they want them to do. Once your pet has latched on to the fact that you can communicate with them in this way they will very quickly respond to your messages.

Rescuing lost pets

Sometimes our animal friends go missing, for all sorts of different reasons. This particularly applies to cats, which need to explore their world, and this curiosity can sometimes get them into all sorts of scrapes. If you are worried about your cat or dog there is a simple exercise that you can do both to protect them and let them know that it is time they came back to you. The Ancient Egyptian cat goddess is called Bast or Bastet. She is depicted either as a woman with a cat's head or as a cat sitting upright. If it is a cat that you need to contact you can imagine it sitting between the paws of this being, and then place a golden collar with a lead attached around their neck. Bast will

help and protect them if they have been trapped or
injured. To get them to return, gently tug on the golden
cord and visualise them coming back home. This will
convey to them your concern.

Dogs, being more dependent, do not normally go
'walkabout' for any length of time, but the same principles
apply, although in this case I would invoke the Egyptian
jackal god Anubis.

Wild animals and other species

As I have stated, domestic animals and those that associate
with people, such as pets, are among the more spiritually
evolved species on the planet, because they are learning
both to individualise and relate to another species. Other
highly intelligent creatures like whales and dolphins can
also be ranked in this group. Such creatures help with the
balance of the energies of the planet, and are very attuned
to its psychic matrix. The slaughter of these creatures for
profit is a very sad reflection on humanity's inability to
appreciate the hugely valuable role that these beautiful
cetaceans play in the balance of the oceans.

Birds are another group that can house some highly
evolved spirits. The songs of birds are expressions of finer
levels of energy transferred down on to a physical plane.
Through these songs they are expressing their joy to the
Divine, which in turn blesses all that hear and experience
these sounds. Of course, their music is also used for
communication within their species and can express a
wide range of feelings, which the sensitive ear can begin to
discern.

There are many species on this planet which do not
normally interact with human beings, yet all have their
role in helping maintain an ecological balance. We are in
a period when many species are disappearing. Such extinc-
tions do occur naturally when the physical cycle has run
its course, but we need to be very careful about speeding

up this process through our ignorance and not destroying our wonderful birthright.

Shamanic association with animals

Animals often appear in the inner world of the shaman, or indeed anyone engaged in exploring the inner reaches of their minds. Animals such as bears, eagles, lions and so on help us connect with the different qualities that these creatures embody. The appearance of specific animals in one's outer world can also herald a significant event.

I once attended what turned out to be a very difficult meeting in which I was to lose my job, and on the way there I met a snake. I was walking along a pathway when this snake came out of a wall on my right, crossed my path and went into some grass on my left. 'A snake in the grass!' The meaning was clear, and this event forewarned me of what was to happen.

The following exercise will help you connect with one of your power animals. These change as you grow so as you repeat the exercise on different occasions you will meet new animals in the process. It is also important to remember that the animal sent to you is the one that is right for you, even if your intellect says otherwise. Sometimes people receive very humble or tiny creatures which they feel are beneath them or are repugnant in some way. Be brave yet humble and gratefully receive whatever is offered you. There is always a reason, and by tuning into yourself you will discover that reason.

Connecting to Your Power Animal
Aim: To learn how to access your power animal
Time: 5–10 minutes

Find a place where you can be quiet and will not be disturbed and then carry out the Earth Attunement Exercise given in Chapter 1.

1. Connect to the Sun and ask the Sun to send you an animal companion to help you in your spiritual work.

2. You should then become aware of an animal travelling down the sunbeam of light to your feet, or close to your body.

3. When the animal arrives, greet it and then stretch out your hand in your imagination and feel its coat, gently stroking it and sensing what qualities it has to offer you.

4. Find a position where the animal can comfortably be with you – for example, walking beside you, flying overhead, sitting on your shoulder, depending on the animal in question.

5. Try to establish a name for your animal companion so that you can more easily connect with it.

6. Finally thank the animal and bring yourself back to full waking consciousness.

As you go about your daily tasks, imagine that this animal is with you, looking out for your best interests in any way that it can.

Chapter 6
The Deva, Elemental and Angelic Realms

Elemental kingdoms

We now come to a group of beings that we can neither see nor feel in a direct sense, although their forms of expression are all around us in the elements of earth, water, air and fire. We call these beings elementals, although they are also known as Faeries and are inhabitants of the Faerie realms. Many traditional cultures have sensed the presence of spirits in nature; indeed, one major religion – Shinto, from Japan – specifically worships the spirits of place, called Kami, which reside in rocks and caves. The beings that inhabit these realms are conscious like you and I, although obviously they have a very different way of connecting with the physical world that we see around us.

Unless you possess clairvoyant vision you will not readily 'see' the beings that lie behind these seemingly inert elements, although they are very attracted to the innocence of young children and sometimes appear to them, so the child that claims to have seen a 'fairy' may indeed be telling the truth. With a little practice it is quite possible to sense their presence, and if you are lucky to see them clairvoyantly; it is then possible to begin to communicate with these beings. Fortunately myths and traditions give us glimpses into these realms, and I have been blessed with the cooperation and friendship of elementals from each of these domains, with which I have worked now for more than 20 years.

Spirits of the four elements

The spirits of the elements are divided into four categories – earth, water, air and fire. Let us look at each of them in turn.

1. **EARTH:** Earth spirits, that is the beings that relate to rocks, stones, minerals, precious gems, hills and mountains, are traditionally called gnomes. All aspects of the solid physical structure of the planet come within their domain. Although they can be found within rocks, they also have a freedom to move around, but generally they stay close to the ground.

2. **WATER:** Water spirits are connected with all liquids, but their presence can be felt in a much more powerful way by streams, rivers, lakes and, of course, the sea. They are traditionally known as undines, or ondines, although stories of mermaids and mermen are also accounts of these beings.

3. **AIR:** The spirits of the air are connected to all gaseous substances and are best sensed in winds and breezes. Because air moves so quickly they can be difficult to pin down. They are traditionally known as sylphs, although the perception of a 'fairy' with tiny wings that can fly is a close approximation to how they appear to children.

4. **FIRE:** Fire spirits can be found in volcanoes in nature but also in any fire, from candle to inferno. They are known as salamanders or Vulcanii, and are

the most difficult of all of the elementals to connect with, being said to associate only with philosophers and adepts of the magical arts.

The connection that these beings have with the physical world is very different from the way that our spirits link to the physical. There is a relationship through resonance, but these beings are not tied to the physical form in the same way that we are. It is true that a rock may be inhabited by an Earth being or gnome, but it is more a case of that place being his or her home rather than their being tied there for as long as the rock or the stone endures. They move home from time to time just as we do. Fire elementals can be present in a room or place without the physical expression of their element, as can all elementals.

Elemental associations

The four spirits of the elements also represent four principles, which are reflected in many aspects of life. Some of the relationships are as follows:

1. **Earth:**
   a. Human – physical body
   b. Direction – north
   c. Musical instrument – drum
   d. Animal – bull
   e. Symbols – pentangle, crystals. Playing cards – spades. Tarot cards – pentacles
   f. Archangel – Uriel
   g. Qualities – steadfast, enduring, possessive, rhythmical, stubborn, protective, loyal

2. **Water:**
   a. Human – emotions

   b. Direction – west

   c. Musical instrument – strings

   d. Animal – man

   e. Symbol – chalice. Playing cards – hearts. Tarot cards – cups

   f. Archangel – Gabriel

   g. Qualities – flowing, reflective, feeling, meditative, joyous, alluring, seductive, gentle

3. Air:

   a. Human – mental activity, thought

   b. Direction – east

   c. Musical instrument – woodwind

   d. Animal – eagle

   e. Symbols – winged disc, feather. Playing cards – clubs. Tarot cards – swords

   f. Archangel – Raphael

   g. Qualities – freedom-loving, changeable, loves speed, capricious, vibrant, ever moving

4. Fire:

   a. Human – spirit (which is why we light a candle when meditating)

   b. Direction – south

   c. Musical instrument – brass

   d. Animal – lion

   e. Symbol – lighted candle. Playing cards – diamonds. Tarot cards – wands

   f. Archangel – Michael

   g. Qualities – energetic, fiery, powerfully protective, martial, aggressive, burns up and dies down

Elemental evolution

Like all spirit essences these beings commence their evolutionary cycle with a choice as to the way they wish to explore physicality. They also have the additional option of choosing which 'element', be it earth, air, fire or water, they want as their starting point; whether to start their spiritual journey as a gnome, sylph, undine or salamander.

Elementals evolve through first learning to manipulate and understand their own element before progressing to embody the qualities of another element. For example, an earth elemental or gnome that is associated with a group of rocks by the seashore may eventually come to understand and appreciate the role of the undines or water beings. This development process continues until eventually all four elements are assimilated, at which stage the elemental being is called a 'deva'.

Devas

This is a Sanskrit word, from the Hindu tradition, which literally means 'shining one'. However, Christian, Judaic and Islamic cultures know these beings as angels, which include the cherubim and seraphim. It is sometimes confusing today when people run courses about connecting with your guardian angels, for in these cases we are dealing with *Homo sapiens* spirits and not those connected with the deva and elemental kingdoms.

Once devahood has been gained the elemental or angelic being takes on greater and greater responsibilities, looking after whole areas of land or sea and becoming responsible for groups of spirits, which are part of its retinue. There are devas that look after towns and cities as well as tracts of the countryside. At the top of this metaphoric tree is the Planetary Deva, which many people nowadays have come to call Gaia. We will return to this being shortly, but before doing so let us look in greater depth at how we can cooperate with the deva and elemental kingdoms.

Communicating with elementals

Elementals communicate with us through telepathic images, presenting information about the things they know and understand. I have run many courses showing people how they can communicate with these realms. In the first instance you need to believe in their existence. This can be hard for those people brought up in a very rational way. Once the bridge has been crossed there is a rich world waiting to be explored.

Over the centuries we have created a picture of how these elemental beings look, and these images get fed back to us. For example, gnomes are traditionally seen as small human-like beings one to three feet tall, much as portrayed in the traditional 'garden gnome'. If they presented an image to us of, say, a golden rock, we might not identify it as an elemental spirit. In a similar way a fire elemental would be more likely to show itself as a fiery being rather than a bright 'spark of light'. They present mental images to us that reflect our understanding of their domains. They not only read our minds but are also acutely conscious of our feelings and spiritual awareness. A person who lacks respect for nature will never gain their sympathy or support.

We do not appreciate how clearly these emotional qualities show up in our individual energy fields, which can be easily read by spirit essences. So to gain the respect and help of the elemental kingdoms you have to love nature.

Elemental communication

During the course of one workshop I asked a water elemental being to go around each of the participants in turn and sit on their hands. One lady first saw a clear rock crystal, which then dissolved into a swirling mass of energy before becoming like a fine mist. As I had not said which element I would call upon she was perplexed at what she had picked up. In this instance the water spirit was conveying to her through picture images the transition it goes through from ice to water to steam. She had clearly perceived this as she was very sensitive.

In another instance a friend was listening to me talk at a workshop, outdoors, where we were learning to communicate with the elemental beings. He was suddenly aware of two gnomes standing close by, listening to what I was saying. Noticing that they were quite small, he mentally said to them, 'Why are you so small?' They immediately grew to an enormous size, like giants, and asked him whether he was happy now. Being over six feet tall himself, my friend was quite amazed. They then shrank back to the size they had been before and said that they adopted the size that suited them best.

The following exercise will start the process of helping you communicate with the elemental realms.

Elemental Attunement Exercise

Aim: To begin the process of learning to communicate with elemental beings

Time: 20–30 minutes

To carry out this exercise you will need to go out into nature. Find a place where you can sit quietly – in a garden, park or wood. If you want particularly to communicate with undines or water beings, you will need to be beside a stream, lake or sea; for fire spirits you can build a bonfire.

1. Close your eyes and try to allow your imagination full rein. Be aware of experiences through all your senses – what you see inwardly in your imagination, what you hear, what feelings you experience, and what you sense through your body.

2. Imagine that your heart is a bright yellow marigold that is opening up and send out your feelings of love to nature, asking for the beings around you to make their presence felt.

3. Trust your perceptions and act on what you experience. So, for example, if you imagine that there is a gnome standing beside you, start to talk to it and try to hear inwardly or clairaudiently its replies.

4. Try not to be impatient if you do not appear to get any immediate response. The nature kingdoms are there; it is just that we have so detuned our sensitivity that it is difficult for many people to readjust to this new level.

Once this process has been started there will be opportunities for communicating with the nature kingdoms whenever you are in a park, garden or woodland. As you continually send out your love through your heart, these kingdoms will hear and respond to you, dancing alongside you in your walks. Patient perseverance will bring its rewards.

Healing the Earth

Trying to heal different Earth energy situations without the aid of the elemental kingdoms is rather like trying to carry out surgery blindfolded, using just the sense of touch. These beings are intimately aware of what is going on energetically on the planet, so their help is of inestimable value. You will need first of all to be open to these realms through your heart, and one of the first places to start can be in working with crystals.

Many people today acquire crystals as an aid to this connection. I sometimes wonder how many stop and think about how the crystal arrived in the shop or stall to be available for purchase. If you have a crystal I suggest that you go and pick it up and for a few minutes feel its energy, or at least the energy of the place where it was mined. Over many years I have rarely sensed a feeling of well-being from such places, and very often the crystals themselves are quite traumatised. Indeed, in some cases I have felt outrage and anger from the elemental forces because of the damage being inflicted on their domains.

Crystals are beautiful, but do not forget that they had a part to play in the landscape in which they originated. Removing the crystals can cause imbalance. One of your first acts, then, if you own a crystal, should be to send a healing thought to the area in which the crystal originated. You can also communicate with the crystal, asking its forgiveness for what has been done to it, but letting it know that the distribution of these semi-precious stones can help people find a new level of respect and understanding for the Earth.

Crystal beings

Very few crystals I have come across in shops or exhibitions have within them a fully developed Earth elemental being. A being can be invited to join your crystal using very similar methods to those used for charging the wand or staff in the section on trees (see pp. 103–4). I would suggest that you take your crystal out into nature, preferably away from people, and place it on the ground. Then ask Gaia, the Spirit of the Earth, for help, telling her why you want to use the crystal and how it might help you in your healing or inner development work. The next step is to invite an elemental being to come into the crystal to work with you. If your intention is sincere your request will be answered, and you will be given a new ally. You will then need to spend time building up a level of trust, and to understand how this particular essence can help you.

Once you are aware of the presence of an elemental spirit that has come to work with you, spend time communicating with it, trying to understand its unique nature and how it can best help you.

How elemental spirits work with us

Once you have begun to build a connection with an elemental spirit it can help you in all sorts of ways. Earth elementals are generally the easiest of all of these beings to contact, with fire being the hardest. However, they are attracted by your inner nature, so that a naturally fiery person will more easily attract a salamander than a person who is very placid.

In the temples of the past, such as those of Ancient Egypt, elemental forces were invited to help with all sorts of tasks. They make excellent psychic guards and their help can be requested when strong protection is needed. For example, gnomes will look after your possessions, while sylphs or air elementals love to ride on the bonnet of your car and will protect you on your journey. People in the past sometimes invoked an elemental spirit into the magic implements with which they worked.

Sacred drum

Many years ago I acquired an African drum from a second-hand music dealer. To take the drum home I placed it on the front passenger seat of my car. During the journey I became very conscious that I was not alone in the vehicle, for some spirit entity resided in the drum. I had not been consciously aware of this when I had first spotted and then purchased it, but in the intimacy of the car I had no doubts. When I eventually returned home I had an opportunity to quietly connect with this Earth elemental spirit, for that is what it was, and to assure it that everything would be fine. I realised then that there must be a tradition in Africa of inviting gnomes or Earth spirits into physical objects such as drums to assist the user. In this case the poor spirit had been ferried all the way from Africa without quite realising what had happened to it. A few words of reassurance helped considerably, and the drum is now in the possession of a friend of mine, who has a deep respect for such gifts.

The types of task that these spirits take on are as follows:

1. **Earth elementals:** Helpful with all forms of protection of property. Very good at finding lost objects. Good at helping you acquire money or material possessions. Helpful in gardening and similar activities.

2. **Water elementals:** Help provide emotional stability, or the ability to deal more openly with emotions. Will help cleanse and purify water. Will protect you or those associated with you when undertaking water activities, such as swimming and sailing.

3. **Air elementals:** Will protect you when travelling, whether by car or plane. Good at helping you find information through books and suchlike and inducing mental clarity.

4. **Fire elementals:** Powerful cleansers and protectors when carrying out Earth healing activities, such as

exorcisms. There is a tremendous power that comes from fire elementals which is very helpful in tackling all types of negative energy situations.

Elemental protectors

A friend of mine who had acquired the help of a fire elemental or salamander was travelling on the Tube late one evening. She was alone in a carriage when an aggressive individual got in and then started to come towards her in a threatening way, demanding that she hand over her bag. She called inwardly for the help of her elemental companion and instantly the man stepped back and started to scream, saying that his face was on fire. At the next station he jumped out of the carriage and disappeared up the platform. My friend was quite unharmed.

If you can build complete trust with beings from these realms you will find that specific elemental spirits will come and work with you and be with you for the rest of your life. Once this occurs your ability to be able to help balance and heal some of the problems on the Earth is enormously increased. These beings will attach themselves to your auric field and, although they can move away from you independently if they choose or if you give them a specific task, they generally stay close by you the whole time. They also benefit from this connection by gaining experiences through you. If this happens to you, do spend time building a rapport with them, asking them to tell you all about their realm and previous experiences.

In my own case my first such companion was an Earth elemental, whom I first encountered more than 25 years ago. His name is Guerrion, and he has been my constant friend and ally ever since. During the course of the following years other spirits have come to join me, the next being an air elemental, followed by a fire spirit and then finally a water spirit. They have been extraordinary companions and helpers in my exploration into their realms, for which I am deeply grateful. Such beings enjoy being given tasks, and there have been many occasions when I have been running courses and workshops when they have been willing to connect with other people to give them direct experience of accessing their realms. Guerrion has become quite a show-off and loves being the centre of attention when asked to make his presence felt.

I have, on occasion, found elemental beings that have been commanded against their will to enter physical objects such as a totem staff. Such actions will ultimately only rebound on their perpetrator. Spirits such as these need to be set free and allowed to continue their evolutionary cycle unhampered by such constraints.

Building a connection with elemental spirits can be great fun; they can be mischievous, reflecting the childlike qualities in all of us. Working with these beings is a very important first step, and you will not be able to win the cooperation of the deva kingdoms until this first stage has been achieved. As at school, the basics need to be dealt with first of all before you progress to higher things.

Spiritual hierarchies

Planetary Devas

As mentioned in the previous section, the evolution of an elemental spirit can eventually lead to it becoming a Planetary Deva, in other words a spirit that is in charge of the evolution of a whole planet – quite a responsibility!

Each planet in this solar system has its Planetary Deva, which generates the influence that astrologers detect. Even though from our perspective these planets do not hold any life, in fact vast numbers of spirits do exist on and around each of our planetary neighbours, although only in very few cases do spirits incarnate down to the same level of physicality that we experience here on Earth.

There is a slightly less dense level of incarnation that interacts with the physical world which is sometimes referred to as the 'etheric plane'. If we could 'see' on this dimension we would be aware of as many different life forms as we experience life here on Earth, at the dense physical level at which we understand life to exist. This is the source of many of the portrayals of mythological creatures found around the world. The Ancient Greeks were very conscious of these other domains and described them in great detail in their myths.

Solar Logos

The pinnacle of spiritual life in this solar system resides in the Sun – a being sometimes called the 'Solar Logos' which is responsible for all spiritual experience within this solar system in the evolutionary journey back to God. From the information relayed to me this Great Spirit has incarnated on two occasions in a human body, which it was able to do by stepping down its energy. The first incarnation was during a period of prehistory, but the second was as the man we know as Jesus, when this spirit tried to set humanity on a new path of selfless loving. The Christ spirit could easily have stopped the crucifixion, but had it done so the karmic backlash against those spirits that wished to suppress what He came to do would have been enormous, for when two forces meet the damage inflicted on the loser always reflects the power of the stronger. So this spirit chose instead to surrender its life in the way we know so well. Sadly Christianity, as we know it today, has deviated quite considerably from the original teachings of Christ.

When the Solar Logos manifested itself in this way, the whole planet was touched by its energy and benefited from the experience. The Buddha was an incarnation of the

Planetary Deva of Neptune, while Moses fulfilled the same role from Mars. Our own planet also has its Planetary Deva, which in recent times has come to be known as Gaia.

Gaia – our Planetary Deva

My first awareness of this spirit came in the early 1970s when I was carrying out a meditation with a small group of friends focused on healing the Earth. During the meditation I was suddenly aware of a spirit that came and stood to the left of the group. She appeared as a mature woman, clothed in a pale green gown that reached down to the floor. There was a wonderful warmth and depth that emanated from her, but all she said to me was 'I am the Earth mother and my name is Gaia'. She stayed to the end of the meditation and then quietly withdrew.

At that stage I had no idea who Gaia was, this being a couple of years before Jim Lovelock's book on the Gaia hypothesis was published. So I had to refer to my books of mythology to discover that this was the name that the Ancient Greeks gave to the Earth mother goddess.

Through the meditation I had inadvertently connected to her consciousness and she had responded by projecting an image to which I could relate. The computer offers a simple analogy to explain how this happens. Today we can send images to each other through a computer link-up. We know that what we see on the screen is a two-dimensional image of the person and not the person themselves. And so it is when we connect to beings from these higher dimensions – what they project back to us is simply a means of communicating with them in a way that we can comprehend. Gaia is not a person, but the only way my mind at the time could comprehend what she was conveying was through her appearance in a guise that I would recognise.

Gaia is the deva responsible for this Earth and her spirit is everywhere. It is perhaps strange that we should relate this spirit to the Earth, for according to Murry Hope, in her book *The Gaia Dialogues*,[†††] she started her experiences as a water elemental at a period in the evolution of the universe way before this solar system was formed. It is a concept with which I would agree based on my own subsequent communications with this being. It is also really a mistake to call her 'she', for the Earth Spirit embodies both halves of a polarity. At the moment we tend to relate more to this feminine part because of the increased dominance of the feminine principle at the moment. However, the masculine half, which the Ancient Egyptians called Geb, is equally important. If we are to find proper balance in this world we need to acknowledge and honour both principles, for they are equally significant. If we focus only on one half of the spirit we will create an imbalance. This happened within Christianity, which established a Trinity (Father, Son and Holy Ghost) in which the feminine is absent. This exaggerated the masculine qualities, at the expense of the feminine, which led to some of the travesties carried out in the name of this religion.

Connection with Geb

When we carry out Earth healing work it is very important that we feel a connection with both the masculine and feminine aspects of our Planetary Deva, and ask for help for what we are trying to achieve. When I first came to connect with the masculine aspect of the deva, he appeared in the guise of the Egyptian god Geb, standing as a giant, at least 20 feet tall. I was, in effect, linking to him in the way the Ancient Egyptians did; for them the gods and goddesses were always seen as giants. This is why, in various Egyptian scenes, the pharaoh, who was perceived as a god incarnate, is always shown as being much taller

---

[†††]Hope, Murry, *The Gaia Dialogues*, Thoth Publications (1995).

than his subjects. For simplicity, then, I would suggest that you adopt the terms Geb and Gaia for the twin masculine and feminine aspects of our Planetary Deva. Both need to be honoured together, for we exist on this Earth through their sanction.

Gaia/Geb is responsible for the evolutionary development of all life on this planet, from the humblest microbe to we human beings. Our Planetary Deva allows all species to explore their gift of free will, although there are certain limitations which, from time to time, they can and do impose. Should human beings ever reach a point where there was a danger of destroying this planet, and this is quite possible, then powerful forces would be brought to bear to prevent this occurring.

It was Gaia/Geb who determined when the age of the dinosaurs should be brought to an end by invoking an agent of destruction in the form of a comet, which brought with it a whole range of new energies that were important for the evolutionary development of our world. The spirits of the dinosaurs have continued on their journey of spiritual evolution, although some, which had not finished their physical experiences, subsequently incarnated into other reptilian creatures, and also birds.

The great god Pan

While Gaia/Geb is the deva of this planet, nature itself comes under the guardianship of another being, called Pan. The name is derived from Greek myths, where Pan was usually depicted as a man with a horned head and the legs of a goat, playing his pan pipes as he danced through the woods. Sadly, because of their desire to distance themselves from pagan beliefs, he has become equated with the 'Devil' in many Christian depictions, particularly in medieval paintings, where the Devil is shown as a goat-legged man with cloven hoofs and horned head. Nothing could be further from the truth, for Pan expresses only gentleness and wisdom. He is a highly evolved being working with Gaia/Geb on the development of the Earth.

Such beings can communicate with us if we are but open to them. What we perceive inwardly is a reflection of their energy stepped down to our level of understanding. Pan loves to dance in nature, and you may be lucky one day to hear the wonderful melodies of his pan pipes. A beautiful description of Pan is given in the book *Findhorn Garden*,[‡‡‡] in which a certain 'Roc' Abercrombie describes his meeting with this being in Attingham Park, Shropshire.

> I became aware of Pan walking by my side and of a strong bond between us. He stepped behind me then walked into me so that we became one, and I saw the surroundings through his eyes. At the same time, part of me – the recording, observing part of me – stood aside. The experience was not a form of possession but of identification, a kind of integration.
>
> The moment he stepped into me the woods became alive with a myriad of beings – elementals, nymphs, dryads, fauns, elves, gnomes, fairies and so on, far too numerous to catalogue. They varied in size from tiny beings a fraction of an inch in height – like the ones I saw swarming about on a clump of toadstools – to beautiful elfin creatures three or four feet tall. Some of them danced around me in a ring; all were welcoming and full of rejoicing. The nature spirits love and delight in the work they do and express this in movement.
>
> I felt as if I were outside time and space. Everything was happening in the now. It is impossible

---

[‡‡‡]The Findhorn Community, *The Findhorn Garden*, Turnstone Books (1975).

to give more than a faint impression of the actuality of this experience, but I would express the exultation and the feeling of joy and delight. Yet there was an underlying peace, contentment and a sense of spiritual presence ... When I had almost reached the spot where the experience had started, the heightened awareness began to fade and Pan withdrew, leaving me once more my ordinary self.

The archangels Michael and Lucifer

Planetary Devas are at the same evolutionary level as, and can be equated with, the archangels of Christian and Islamic tradition. Indeed, Raphael is the Planetary Deva of Mercury, while Michael is helping our own deva, Gaia/Geb, counter the Luciferic energies that surround this planet at the moment. Archangels are beings that have reached a very high level of spiritual evolution but not quite the level of God consciousness, and they are therefore not perfect.

Lucifer is an archangel who turned away from God and has been responsible for encouraging the negative shadow aspects of human nature. Sadly, when a spirit of this magnitude stepped onto the shadow path, to work with what the Star Wars films called the 'dark' side of the Force, there were many spirits that followed him and now form part of his retinue – the fallen angels. They work to try to exaggerate all the destructive, fear-driven aspects of human nature.

From time to time one or other of the Luciferic agents have incarnated as a human being to stir up strife and enmity, such as occurs in warfare, which is the fuel that feeds these negative forces. More generally they operate through the minds of those who allow fear, bigotry, intolerance, hatred and revenge to dominate their lives.

Lucifer is linked to our Moon and has been able to use some of the lunar energies in his malign influence, which is one of the reasons why increased criminal activity takes place at the time of the full moon. This is not to say, however, that all lunar influences are malign.

Hallmarks of Luciferic influence

Some people ask me how they can tell whether a teaching, philosophy or individual is working with Luciferic energy. There is a very simple test that can be applied, which can be summed up under four headings. If any of these apply then look very closely at what is being offered, for I would suspect that the teaching, religion or philosophy in question is tainted in some way. The headings are:

1. **Fear** – the introduction of fear in any way or at any level

2. **Ego** – the inflation of the ego

3. **Intolerance** – intolerance of, or feeling of superiority over, others

4. **Free will** – does the teaching inhibit your free will, your capacity to think for yourself?

The fear element can be introduced in a very subtle way. For example, you might be informed that your spiritual development will be held back if you do not adhere to what is being asked of you. This happened to me many years ago when I attended a channelling purporting to come from the Master (i.e. Christ). The fear element was introduced when I was told that if I did not agree to what I was being asked (ordered) to do then I would suffer karmically. This was not even subtly put but openly expressed. Needless to say, I did not go along with this, but others not so wary could easily have fallen into the trap.

The ego is always fair game in any such insidious entrapment. Exploiting it can take the form of a statement such as 'You have been specially selected because of your spiritual evolution' or one to the effect that your group has some 'special purpose'. Always look very carefully when such statements are made to you.

Any intolerance of other beliefs, expressions of superiority to fellow men and women or claims of belonging to the 'elect' are certainly an alignment, at some level, with those aspects that are anti-God. Believe what you believe and rejoice in it, but also honour and acknowledge the beliefs of others, for we are all spirits evolving on a wonderful journey back to our Creator.

Finally, while spiritual discipline is necessary, be wary of those teachings which inhibit your free will, your ability to think for yourself, forcing you to believe what is being offered.

The fact that any of these four elements – fear, ego, intolerance and the inhibition of free will – is present in the religious or spiritual teachings that you encounter does not mean that all aspects of the teaching are flawed. These elements can certainly be found in some of the more extreme fundamentalist expressions of Christianity, Judaism, Islam and Hinduism. The challenge to these groups and institutions is to let go of these controlling elements, to find the truth of their own beliefs and to acknowledge that others may wish to follow a different path, which also has its inherent truths.

Uriel, Gabriel and Raphael

Uriel, Gabriel and Raphael, the other well-known archangels, are emissaries of the Solar Logos. Uriel is sometimes called the light of God and is associated with revelation. Gabriel was the archangel who appeared to Mary to announce the birth of Jesus and who instructed

Muhammad. Raphael is the archangel of healing, and it is claimed that it was his energy which stirred the waters in the pool of Bethesda in the biblical story.

Many people today invoke these archangelic presences in their healing work. All that is necessary is to send a thought, or say out loud words such as: 'I call upon the archangels Michael, Uriel, Gabriel and Raphael to protect, inspire and guide me with this healing work.'

When you invoke any spirits in this way, they also need to be dismissed at the end of the healing session with words such as: 'I thank the archangels Michael, Uriel, Gabriel and Raphael for their over-lighting presence. May they return to their own in love and peace. Go in peace.'

Other spiritual beings of our Earth

Before we conclude this chapter, something needs to be said about some of the other spiritual energies that you might experience in your explorations into these realms. Myths are wonderful sources of information on these different realms, because those who created the myths were not so limited in their perspectives as we have tended now to become. They depicted what they experienced in all its richness and variety. Today, unless we can put something into a test tube and measure it, the common perception, among scientists particularly, is that it does not exist. Nothing could be further from the truth.

Each of these beings relates to one or other of the elemental forces. I will look at them in the order of fire, air, water and earth. It should be appreciated that, while a deva has assimilated the qualities of each of the other elements, it maintains its inherent original quality, at least to begin with. It is rather like moving to a foreign country. You might learn all the customs of your new land but you would still retain the qualities of your country of origin.

And so it is with spirits that become devas; their earthiness or wateriness and so on will still shine through.

Dragons

Fire has always been regarded as the most powerful of all the elemental forces. Although they also embody all the other elemental qualities, dragons are basically fire devas, and fulfil a variety of roles on this planet. This does not mean to say that they need a physical fire to manifest themselves, for being devas they can move freely around the planet, although they are likely to congregate near volcanoes.

To command dragon energy an individual must have gone through many initiatory processes and be working at a very high level. The myth of St George slaying the dragon is effectively the story of an individual mastering this level of initiation. It may seem strange that we should use the analogy of slaying something, but at a spiritual level you can never slay anything, only transform it, or more accurately transform your relationship with it. These forces can be great protectors and help extensively with healing different imbalances on this planet.

Trapped dragon

Many years ago I was involved in releasing a dragon that had been trapped through occult rituals by a group of priests in the Middle Ages. This dragon spirit lived under the hill of a town in southern France called Le Castellet. During the thirteenth century this fortified place had been used by a group of Knights Templar, who had invoked and worked with its energies. Following the overthrow of this military order, a group of priests had visited the site and carried out various rituals to seal and chain this dragon energy by symbolically driving a stake through its heart. As I have stated, you cannot slay anything at this level, so the dragon was trapped and in a great deal of agony. With the help of a few friends we were able to break this curse and release the dragon, which was most grateful.

Valkyries

The Valkyries of Teutonic mythology are air devas. Traditionally they were seen as maidens accompanying Odin on his journeys, and played a role in conveying the spirits of the warrior heroes into Valhalla, the Teutonic heaven. In my experience air devas, because of their rapid movements, are not as easy to contact as the devic beings from the other elements. If you are a person in tune with airy things – for example, you like fast cars and are quick-thinking – you may be lucky. But generally considerable patience is required to connect with these spirits and their energies, which most dramatically manifest themselves through storms or hurricanes.

Christ displayed his mastery of these elements when he commanded the storm, 'Peace, be still,' and immediately the winds abated. In more recent times it was the assistance of the wind devas or Valkyries which allowed British troops in the Second World War to be evacuated from Dunkirk, in France, during three days of perfectly calm weather. This miracle was no accident but occurred through cooperation with the landscape devas of Britain, which had been invoked, by those working spiritually at this level, for our protection.

Two of the elemental forces, water and earth, are generally regarded as negative, in a yin sense, in that they respond to the other energies that impact upon them. Fire and air are positive, in that the devas and elemental beings behind these elements are actively moving the forces at their disposal. Science tries to suggest that this is all part of Chaos Theory, according to which the beating of a butterfly's wings in one part of the world causes a hurricane in another.

There are principles that air elementals follow, but science will not be able to accurately predict what is going to happen to, say, long-term weather patterns until human beings have learned how to communicate and cooperate with the devic forces. The same is true for the element of fire, when lightning or volcanic activity take place. These are triggered by the conscious wishes of this realm. The seemingly destructive fire that rages through a forest is clearing and cleansing the area for new life, and is undertaken as an act of cooperation between the different kingdoms. A time will come in the future when human beings and the devic realms will conduct a dialogue together and the more destructive aspects of nature will be considerably diminished. At the moment the reverse is taking place, for these realms are trying to awaken human beings to the results of our polluting activities. Sadly, sometimes violent action is the only thing which shakes us out of our inertia or lethargy.

Devas of the lakes, seas and rivers

Human beings are made up of over 70 per cent water, and it is not without accident that this element is also very important to us. In the four creatures of the Evangelists in the Bible – the lion, the bull, the eagle and man – each element is represented: fire by the lion, earth by the bull, air by the eagle and water by man, which suggests that human beings and water have a special affinity.

So why is water so important to us? Water works through our emotions and also holds memories of all that has occurred on this planet. When we drink a glass of water we are taking into ourselves the memory patterns of

everything that the water has experienced, and these
patterns pass through us, incorporating also our own
memory patterns, which are then excreted back into the
Earth. This is why drinking recycled water is far from
ideal; even though it has been technically cleansed, the
memories are still there. Spring water is much more
vibrant and beneficial.

Myths present us with many different images of
water elemental and devic beings. The great god of the
seas is Neptune, from the Roman myths, whom the
Ancient Greeks knew as Poseidon. His retinue comprises
many fabulous creatures, some of which you might experience when you start to understand and harmonise with
these realms. Places like Finland, with its wonderful lakes,
provide a valuable opportunity for connecting with these
kingdoms, which can help in providing us with much-
needed inner peace and balance.

Water pollution is a serious problem, for it affects the
link between the spiritual essence and its physical structure. Indeed, all pollution has the same impact in different
ways. If you cause disease in the body it creates imbalance
within the spirit. Collectively we have a great karmic
responsibility not to create pollution, and when it does
occur to do everything in our power to rebalance and heal
distorted energies. Communicating with the water devas
will help you become aware of the imbalances in the lakes,
rivers, streams or seas in your locality, to which you can
then send healing thoughts.

Elementals marrying mortals

Devas of the seas were known as Nereids to the Ancient
Greeks. On occasion the myths tell us that they have come
forth from their own realm to marry mortal men, and from
the union a magical or golden child is born. This underlines
the connection that we have with these watery realms.

Indeed, it is possible for a deva or elemental to incarnate as a human being, although this rarely occurs. Such events happen when there is a particular task to perform, assisting Gaia/Geb in the development of human beings on this planet. Such a spirit might introduce a new form of music, art or literature. The great Finnish composer Sibelius was an incarnate deva, which was why he was able to capture the essence of the elemental forces so powerfully through his music. Churchill was another incarnate devic spirit, on this occasion come to counter the 'occult' forces that were invoked in Germany through the Nazi regime.

Giants

Earth giants tend to appear like human beings because that is how we have traditionally related to them, but they are basically devic spirits of the Earth. Like dragons they embody all four elements, but they tend to remain in fixed places, being associated with hills and mountains and special places in the landscape. They are sources of great wisdom if you can begin to connect with them, and can help by offering insights into what needs to be done to heal or rebalance the energies of a particular area.

Human beings, for all our versatility, cause many problems in the energetic balance of places. This is redeemed in part by our working with plants and trees in our gardens, but there are many areas, in Britain and elsewhere in the world, which need a great deal of attention. If you can become aware of the Earth giants of your locality and communicate with them, they will tell you what needs to be done in this respect.

Amoral elementals

One of the important gifts we can offer to the elemental forces on this planet is a greater spiritual awareness of moral virtue. By their nature, elemental forces are amoral and have no sense of the impact of what they do. Life and death to them have no meaning in the way they do to us.

In consequence a violent hurricane can quite happily rip up plants and trees from the ground without any awareness of the impact that this has on these life forms. The same is true of violent earthquakes and volcanic activity, which can wreak so much havoc. In trying to communicate openly with these different realms, we can beneficially learn from each other.

Trolls, demons, goblins and banshees

It would be inappropriate to complete this section without making reference to a whole range of negative or destructive elemental beings that have been mentioned in fairy tales and folk tradition, or more recently in such stories as *Lord of the Rings* and *Harry Potter*. Do such beings really exist?

I have been exploring the Faerie and magical realms for more than 30 years, and far and away the largest group of malefic energies I have met has stemmed from human activity. There have been places where the elemental forces have been very unhappy and quite sullen in their attitudes towards me, but when I enquired further of them I discovered that they had good reason, because of some human activity carried out in the past.

This could take many forms, from a total disregard of their kingdoms to the deliberate invocation of demonic forces in a particular spot through occult or magical rituals. If I discover the latter to be true then I carry out any necessary cleansing work, apologising to my elemental friends for the crassness of human beings. Their responses have always been of unalloyed joy that someone has tried to listen to and understand them.

Nature has a reflective face. If our attitudes towards

these realms are filled with suspicion and fear then this is what we will discover mirrored back at us. We will be confronted by some of the hideous creatures of the elemental realms. They are only reflecting our own negativity. If we approach nature with an open, loving heart, then we will only ever be blessed by the elementals' responses. They want and need human contact. There is so much we can learn from them if only we make the effort.

EARTH HEALING

Part 2

Chapter 7

Healing the Subtle Energies of Places

In this chapter we will look at how you can start the process of changing and balancing disturbed subtle energies within places. In Chapter 10 we will explore how physical energies, such as electromagnetism, affect us, but here we will be dealing with non-physical energies.

Disturbed energies

All human activity generates an influence that flows out from us like the ripples formed when a pebble is thrown into a pond. Most of the time these energies are inconsequential in that they do not create any real problems. They can be beneficial to the planet and our environment if our intentions are good; however, we only have to look around our world to realise that in some instances very disturbed energy patterns have been and are still being created, such as those produced by warfare and killing. In the fullness of time all these disturbed energies will need to be cleansed and rebalanced, but this will not happen overnight because this type of cleansing work is quite specialist and, in the more severe cases, is best tackled by a group of people rather than a single individual.

During the course of the next few chapters we will look at the range of problems that you might confront and how you can start to effectively balance, albeit in a small way, some of the traumas that have been created by human beings on this planet.

Balancing the energy of your home

A good place to start this process is in your own home, discovering what is contained there and then balancing its vibrations. This will not only help your home environment but also all the people who live there, including you.

Just for a moment close your eyes and imagine yourself walking around your house, asking yourself the following questions:

- How do the rooms seem energetically?
- Which rooms or parts of rooms do not feel quite balanced?

When I have asked my students to carry out this exercise for themselves, it has been surprising how often they recognise some problem that they had only been dimly conscious of before.

If you 'feel' your way into the energy of each room in turn you will start to build up a picture, which either feels right or seems problematic in some way. If you are unsure, visualise a pair of scales. Do they balance? If not (which indicates that something is wrong), you can make a mental note of where you sense the problems lie.

Sensing disturbed energies

Everybody is individual, so no two people will get exactly the same response when tuning into the subtle energies of a room or building. Here are a few basic questions that you can ask yourself.

- Does the room or any part of it feel cold?
- Do I get any uncomfortable sensations?
- Do I experience any unpleasant smells?
- Are there any signs of damp, mould, leaks or dirt?
- Do I inwardly see any disturbed images, strange faces or ugly forms?
- Do I hear any strange noises or see apparitions?
- Does the room feel heavy or claustrophobic?
- Do I feel fear or sense the hairs on my head/neck standing up?

All these are examples of what you might experience or feel if the subtle energy is disturbed in any way.

Let us assume to begin with that there is no major difficulty with any of the rooms in your home but that you just wish to clear the influences of the previous occupants of the property and to place a bright new energy there which reflects you. Remember that all mental and emotional activity leaves a trace. If emotional problems have been part of the experience of your home, through its previous occupants, the subtle energies left behind will continue to haunt you. Feng shui consultants, when moving home, will often demand information on the lives of the previous occupants before committing themselves to a purchase for this very reason. The good news is that you do not need to be affected in this way, for whatever has been generated by human thought can be changed, cleansed and balanced by human thought.

Mental tools and weapons

Learning to harness your thought power for healing and self-development is rather like going into a mental gymnasium. You will perhaps be relieved to know that this does not require hours of meditation, although the meditative exercises that have been outlined in this book are important for honing your skills. What is needed is that you use your mind in a positive yang way to tackle areas of imbalance that manifest themselves around you. To help this process there are a number of imaginary tools or weapons that you can visualise yourself possessing which will help with these tasks. This is why a rich imagination is helpful.

One of these is the sword, although Harry Potter fans might prefer a magic wand. An imagined sword or wand pointed at an object is a simple way of focusing and directing your thoughts in a concentrated beam. In this context the Star Wars movies provide some real insight into how 'thought', the power of the 'Force', can be used either creatively or destructively.

To clear and reset the energy of a room you will need to use the sword in combination with the element of fire – in other words to imagine that you have in your hand a flaming sword. Those who have studied mythology will know that this is one of the symbols of the archangel Michael, so by calling on certain magical implements you are also aligning yourself with specific spiritual energies.

My early training took place well before the days of Star Wars movies, so the 'flaming sword' has always been quite natural to me, but I know that some of my students today prefer to imagine that they have a 'light sabre'. Close your eyes for a moment and imagine that you are holding a 'flaming sword' or a 'light sabre' in your hand. How does this feel? Whichever you use, it is important to remember that fire is the primary cleansing and transforming element within the elemental kingdom and its power will remove any negative energies with which it comes into contact.

The following exercise can be carried out in your mind alone or you can perform it in a more direct way, by going into the room in question and physically acting out the different elements. Both work equally well. Some people like to put enormous effort into creating rituals of cleansing which involve the use of incense, physical implements, such as an actual sword, and so on. This might help set the mood but it is entirely unnecessary.

There are many advantages to working through the mind alone, not least because it means that you can always respond immediately whenever your energies are required. You are not dependent on complicated rituals to carry out your healing work. It is also quite possible to cleanse and balance the energies of places from a distance. Indeed, you have probably recognised already that neither time nor space impose any barrier to the power of thought.

If you think of someone or some place, you immediately create a connection with them; the link is opened up instantly, and the only impediment to effecting an exchange of energy is the limitations imposed on your thought power by your beliefs. As Christ demonstrated, if you have faith you can literally move mountains.

Nature abhors a vacuum

The next important point to remember is the simple maxim 'Nature abhors a vacuum'. In other words, if you remove an energy you will need to put something back in its place. The importance of this cannot be over-stressed, for failure to do so could leave the door open for more destructive negative energies to enter. So what is it that we put back? In simple terms you can imagine any symbol with which you feel a positive relationship being placed in the room. This could take the form of a Christian cross, or preferably an equal-armed Celtic cross, because it is more balanced, or even a flower. When I first started doing this type of space clearing I was told to simply plunge my flaming sword into the floor. Today I generally prefer to use broad-based symbols such as the Celtic cross, which signifies the four elements held within the circle of spirit, although I often also use a white rose, which is another of the symbols of the archangel Michael.

White roses

Many years ago I was involved in clearing a property in southern France, and a few days after the event the occupant said that she could still smell the rose essence that we must have sprinkled around the place. She had psychically picked up, through her intuitive sense of smell, the imagined white roses we had planted in each of the rooms, and thought that we must have used actual rose essence. She had difficulty believing us when we assured her that no essence had been used, because to her the scent was so powerful. Some people do have a nose for sensing balanced or disturbed energy, which, in the latter case, generally manifests itself as some unpleasant odour.

Spirit presences

If you sense the presence of a spirit you will need to deal with this first. How to do so is described in the next chapter, but for the moment leave well alone any room where you sense there might be a spirit or earth-bound soul.

Cleansing the Energy of a Room and Setting a New Vibration

Aim: To cleanse and reset the vibrational energy of a room
Time: 10–15 minutes

Find a place where you can be quiet and will not be disturbed. This does not need to be the room that you intend to cleanse, although to begin with it might be easier for you to be there. Sit in a chair with your feet firmly on the ground, or stand if you prefer.

1. Close your eyes and first carry out the exercise for connecting to the Sun and the Earth (see p. 18). Then follow this by putting strong protection around yourself.

2. Ask the Sun whether it is appropriate for you to carry out this clearing work. If you get a strong impression of a 'no' answer, try to find out why. It may just be that there is some problem that needs more understanding or some form of specialist attention. If this is the case, restrict yourself to a room where you do not get a strong 'no' response. We will look at different methods of heightening this sense of awareness in the next chapter.

3. Spend a few moments linking to the spiritual forces of the four elements. By just asking for their help and participation you are beginning to build some valuable bridges into this realm.

4. Connect to the Sun, asking it which symbol would be most suitable for this particular room. If nothing comes through in any strong way, select a symbol and ask whether this is suitable. If you do not receive a clear 'no' then you can assume that it is all right to proceed.

5. Next imagine that you are holding in your hand a 'flaming sword' or, if you prefer, your 'light sabre'. You might even experiment with which feels more appropriate. Sweep around the whole room, in clockwise circles, starting with the sword or sabre at floor level and moving slowly up the walls to the ceiling.

6. Imagine that you are sending all the cleansed and swept energy out through the ceiling into the outer atmosphere of the planet, where it will be transformed and further purified.

7. As soon as this has been done, place the symbol of your choice in the centre of the room and sense that it is radiating energy that fills the whole space with its vibrational essence.

8. Finally, place a protection around the room and thank all the forces of the cosmos for their help.

Your room will now be cleansed and hold a new energy, depending on what you have called upon. You can now proceed to clear and reset the vibrations of all the other rooms in the house, not forgetting the toilets and cupboards. With practice it becomes possible to clear and reset the energies of an entire house in one sweep by imagining that your flaming sword is passing through all the inner walls of the property and you are placing one universal symbol in the centre of the house.

Other properties

This same method can be used on all properties that need rebalancing. However, it is most important that you proceed with great caution when tackling another property, however familiar it might seem to you. You will need to be very mindful of your protections, and I would also strongly urge that you do not work alone. Always have a friend to help whose task can be simply to keep a protection up around you.

Cleansing furniture

Household items such as furniture and jewellery also hold subtle energy. These can be cleansed using the method given above, although on a much smaller scale. Brush down the object with your flaming sword and then place your symbol within it. Remember that second-hand and antique furniture will hold the energies of the previous owners. Moreover, the energies that were part of you 20 years ago may no longer be appropriate today. We do need to move on, so letting go of the past is important.

Another cleanser that you can use for jewellery and small items like crystals is spring water. As has been mentioned, water holds energy and will suck out the memory patterns of what is placed within it. You will need to place the object, such as a crystal, in water for 24 hours to facilitate a full cleansing.

I would also strongly urge that you solicit the help of the water elemental beings when using water in this cleansing way. This can be done quite simply by feeling a connection with their essence as described in Chapter 6 and mentally asking for their assistance.

There are many books on feng shui which cover other valuable aspects of house-balancing work, involving the positioning of furniture and so on. What they offer is worth considering as a complement to the balancing work described here.

Healing from a distance

Cleansing of other places can be performed either by visiting the property or from a distance. There are a number of different ways of cleansing from a distance.

You could imagine that you are flying through the air to the property, or simply projecting you mind into it, and then carrying out the clearing work there, or you could visualise that you are bringing the property to you by transforming the room you are in into one of the rooms of the place you are clearing. Or you could imagine that you are placing a very small version of the property on the floor in front of you, like a doll's house, which can be any size you wish to make it.

You then carry out the clearing using the method given, although in the latter case you do not need to magically reduce yourself to Tom Thumb size to enter each room in turn – you simply sweep your sword through the whole property in one go, as though you were a giant standing over the house. Remember also that the flaming sword is cleansing the atmosphere, not setting the place alight.

You might like to experiment with these three options, adopting the one that feels the most comfortable. However, you will also need to consider the question of protection and whether it is advisable to work alone or with a friend.

I prefer using the first method, projecting my mind into the property, as long as I have a friend or colleague working with me. I ask them to put a protection around me while I carry out the clearing, and we can then change roles. You can always get people to send a protection to you from a distance if they know where and when you will be working. Indeed, I would strongly urge that you do not work alone, except on those places that you know intimately.

The disadvantage of working alone is that you are very vulnerable to a psychic attack if you suddenly discover that there is a real negative presence in the place of which you were unaware when you started. This can and does happen, and may do so even within your own property. I would therefore recommend, if you have to work alone with distant healing, that you adopt the third method, of bringing a small version of the property to you, because in this way you only invoke what you are capable of dealing with. Even then proceed with caution.

It does not matter if two of you work consecutively on the same place, nor if you have several people carrying out the cleansing at the same time. With a group I would always give some people the task of keeping up a protection while the others carry out the clearing work, acting as a team.

Earth healing through sacred sites

The method suggested for distant subtle energy cleansing can be applied to landscape areas. I have often come across places, on walks through the countryside, where the energy feels distorted in some way. Even though I have been working on this type of landscape healing for more than 30 years, unless I feel very sure about the causes and levels of the problem I will always tackle such situations from a distance, tuning into the problem with the help of a colleague to keep up a protection. Experience has taught me that one cannot be too careful.

However, there is another simple yet effective way in which healing can be sent to the Earth – by sending thoughts of balance to a specific local sacred site so that subtle healing energies can be distributed to the landscape as a whole.

Fountain International

An organisation that has done some wonderful work in helping the 'energetic' balance of different areas using this method is the group Fountain International, founded by Colin Bloy. Their approach is both simple and powerful, and has the advantage that the techniques can be applied by both individuals and by groups. For such healing work you first need to establish a point of focus in your environment, which should be a sacred site or other well-known landmark; Fountain International's name is based on the first point of focus they used – the fountain in the centre of Brighton. Healing energy is directed at the chosen location on a regular basis, the idea being that this energy will flow out through any connecting ley lines to bring balance to the specific region.

Great claims are made for the effectiveness of this approach in reducing crime levels and generally improving the quality of life in the area in question. Whether all such claims can be fully substantiated or not I would not wish to assess, but I am very confident that such an approach is beneficial. Like the individual drops that make up the ocean, every little bit helps.

If you do not know of any local sacred sites, then use the place that is closest to you. Centres like Glastonbury Tor in the UK, Ayers Rock (Uluru) in Australia, Mount Shasta in California and the Great Pyramid of Egypt are all internationally known sacred sites and can be used for landscape healing work.

Landscape healing

Below is a simple yet effective exercise that will start you on your journey of Earth healing. It involves sending loving, balancing light 'energy' to a local sacred site. I would suggest that your selected site should be in your locality, somewhere you can easily visit. In time you could choose a location that is further away, or even in another country, by selecting one of the sites given in the Appendix.

There are many potential sites that can act as a focus for this meditation, but I would recommend that to begin with you choose a site that is recognised by other people as being special. If it is a site that has been held sacred over a long period of time, such as an ancient temple, sacred mountain or megalithic site, then so much the better, but this is not absolutely necessary.

What is important is that it is a place where you sense a strong inner connection or resonance. In this you can also be quite specific. For example, if the site you have chosen is a 'beacon' hill, where exactly on the hill do you feel this connection? It might be by a certain tree or rock, or a position with an extensive view. Try to let your intuition guide you to the 'right' spot by asking the Sun and the Earth through the linking meditation to assist you in your selection.

Landscape Healing Meditation Exercise
Aim: To send healing to the landscape through specific sites
Time: 15–20 minutes
Requirements: That you have found and visited a sacred site in your locality which will be the focus of the meditation
Equipment: A lighted candle and incense (optional)

Try to choose a place that has a tradition of being special in some way; that has been held sacred by past generations. There are many possibilities, but suggestions might include a 'beacon' hill or sacred mound; a holy well; a church, synagogue or mosque; a lake; a standing stone; a stone circle or henge and so on.

1. Sit in your usual posture for meditation. If you are on your own you can choose any position suitable. If you are in a group I would recommend that you sit equally spaced in a circle. Light your candle, which should be either in front of you or in the centre of the circle, then carry out the Sun and Earth linking exercise (see p. 18).

2. Next put up your protections as described in Chapter 2. If you are on your own, go to step 5.

3. If you are in a group, first think of the flower energy of your hearts (from the Sun/Earth linking meditation) and then send this energy around the room in a clockwise direction. Try to feel that you are blending your energy with that of the group.

4. Imagine that the energy coming from your heart to the group is a particular colour. Try to be aware of the colours from all the other people; then consciously blend these energies so that the colours begin to merge into a white light.

5. Think of the place that is to be the focus of your meditation and then call upon the energy from the Sun and the Earth and feel this energy flowing through your body and then out from your hands to be focused on the spot that you have chosen. Be very connected to your heart and to feelings of love and balance when doing this work, and then sense or visualise that a shaft of light is flowing into the Earth at this landscape point and then out along the network of energy lines that link to this place.

6. To begin with you do not need to hold this meditation for longer than a minute – much better one minute of concentrated thought than ten minutes of dissipated drift, during which many other thoughts intrude into your mind. The more experienced you are at meditation the longer you will be able to hold your focus, but in any case I would not recommend that you continue sending this energy for more than three minutes. That is quite enough, and it will be effective.

7. Finish by asking for God's blessing for the place selected and then thank the Sun and Earth for the help that you have received.

8. Bring yourself back to full waking consciousness and with your eyes open feel a strong link through your feet to the Earth.

Chapter 8

Spirit Presences and Exorcism

In this chapter we will look at the problems that can arise when a trapped or 'Earth-bound' spirit is held within a place, and the steps that can be carried out to release them.

Spirit presences

Let us suppose that you have detected a spirit in one of the rooms you are cleansing. What do you do? We first need to understand why spirits become trapped before we can consider ways of releasing them.

The near-death experience

In the mid-1970s American doctor Raymond Moody became interested in the stories of some of his patients who had recovered from heart attacks or, in some cases, serious operations. Far from being unconscious at the time, these people reported that they had been aware of all that was taking place around them, although they knew that they were not *in* their bodies but in many cases floating above them or to one side. Moody wrote up these stories in a book called *Life after Life*, which became an immediate best-seller.

Initially the medical establishment viewed these experiences as simple hallucinations with no validity, but some researchers, like Dr Elizabeth Kübler-Ross, tested the veracity of the claims. In an interview I conducted with her many years ago for a film called *Visions of Hope*, based on these extraordinary inner journeys, she told us that she had specifically sought out blind people who had had this experience, which became known as the 'Near-Death Experience', or NDE for short.

Kübler-Ross was able to verify that these blind people could suddenly 'see' quite clearly in this altered state of consciousness and describe accurately what they perceived taking place while 'out of the body'. Other researchers, like Dr Peter Fenwick of the Maudsley Hospital in London, have supported the discoveries of Kübler-Ross and Moody, for NDEs seem to be a widely based phenomenon, which people in all cultures experience.

The first stage of an NDE is being separated from one's body and recognising that consciousness is independent of the physical self. The next step entails passing through what most people describe as a tunnel of light in which they are infused with amazing feelings of love, to a depth and intensity that are almost overwhelming and unlike anything they have ever experienced before.

At the end of the tunnel they describe emerging into a realm where they are often met by relatives or friends whom they know have passed over. Sometimes they see or feel the presence of a great being of light, which gently informs them that this is not the time of their passing and that they have to return to their bodies. The process of returning is often very uncomfortable, for these individuals have been free of all pain and suffering while in this wonderful altered state. On regaining consciousness they recognise that they have gone though a profound life-changing experience, but to begin with hardly dare share what they have encountered.

The journey of the soul at death

The various stages of the NDE tell us what most souls meet when they leave their bodies for the last time through physical death. The first step is the separation from the body where one is fully conscious of one's physical surroundings; the next stage entails travelling through a tunnel of light on to the spiritual planes. This is what should happen, but sometimes, for a whole host of reasons, spirits or souls get stuck between leaving the body and making this transition. What helpers like myself seek to do is to open the door that allows them to access and pass through the tunnel to the place where they will receive all the help and support they need. Once they have made the transition our job is done. They will be well looked after by those spirits whose task it is to receive and welcome those who have just made the journey.

Earth-bound spirits

So why might a spirit get stuck? There are many factors today that influence this transition process. In past times religious concepts powerfully shaped the views of people, and a belief in a life after death was an important ingredient in practically all faiths.

It is not generally appreciated how important our beliefs are. Once you have left the physical body you exist in a realm of *thought* – you create, in effect, your own reality. If you emphatically believe in the finality of death and the extinguishing of consciousness then this is what you will get. I have had to help a number of souls who were, in effect, fast asleep or in an unconscious state simply because of this belief. They had died in their beds, perhaps even while asleep, and their spirits were lying comatose where they had expired. The first step in helping them move on was to send a strong thought to their spirit telling it to wake up. The surprise in some of these spirits is enormous, because they cannot believe that they are still very much alive. I then guide them gently into the tunnel of light so that they can make their transition.

This is not to say that every person who dies without a belief in an after-life gets stuck. It all depends on the evolution of your spirit and the number of previous lives that you have had. An evolved spirit will always be able to override the patterns of the conscious mind at the moment of death.

Another factor is that most people in the past would be very aware when death was approaching, either through illness or when facing foes in physical battle. You saw your enemy and fought him knowing that you might die at any moment. The religious rites carried out before battle helped prepare individuals for this transition.

In the modern world death can come very swiftly in such events as road accidents, for which no preparation has been made. Such an event can cause all sorts of confusion for a spirit, and they can wander lost for quite a period of time.

Major accidents like plane crashes will often spark sympathetic feelings around the world, and there are groups in most countries today who will send healing thoughts to the souls of those caught up in these catastrophic scenarios. This does indeed play an important role in helping those involved in these tragedies make their transition. It is the more local, less media-worthy car crashes and suchlike which can sometimes leave a spirit stuck.

Another scenario that I have come across often involves a deep fear of hell. The concepts of heaven and hell might act as a strong incentive in terms of keeping people to a virtuous path, but they can also act detrimentally in terms of what they go through after death. I have had to deal with many cases of spirits, particularly those from before the nineteenth century, terrified of leaving a house because they believed they were going to go to hell for some past misdeed. In these cases sending a powerful thought of forgiveness was very important before finally releasing them. But is there such a state as hell?

Heaven and hell

The realms beyond our physical world are inhabited by spirits, which exist in a *thought* state. In other words they create their reality through their thoughts, although obviously they are also affected by the thought consciousness of all the other beings around them. If a spirit wishes to experience hell, and many do, then that is what they create for themselves, and they will remain in that state for as long as they choose. It might seem bizarre that a spirit should wish to inflict such suffering upon itself but, as I have already stated, we are our own harshest judges.

Think for a moment what those spirits who carried out the atrocity on the Twin Towers of the World Trade Center building in New York will have to face when they come to terms with what they have done. The only event that occurs with certainty after transition is that a spirit has to face everything it has experienced in its life. It is rather like going to the movies and seeing a replay of your life story, during which you are also very conscious of the thoughts and feelings of the other players on the scene. You will relive all those times when you acted in kindness as well as the moments when you allowed feelings of anger or hatred to dominate your actions. You will see the effects of these actions on others and have a real sense of how they felt.

This can be a very painful experience for a spirit to endure, for it now sees itself for what it really is. Remember that God does not judge, nor do those spirits taking you through this experience judge you. The only person who judges you is yourself, and we are always our harshest critics. You will also be aware again of the karma or life plan you intended to follow and where you missed the plot. This too can be an uncomfortable experience.

Through all this you will receive the loving support of wise beings who want you to progress in a healthy, balanced way. They will advise you about what you might do, but without forcing you to take any particular action. After a period of reflection you may well decide to incarnate again, to put right what you have set in motion in your previous life.

Spirits will often incarnate together over many lives to work through the steps necessary to find harmony and balance. In some cases they will move through a series of lives, being either victim or persecutor until they have reached a point of integration where they can fully accept and balance within themselves these two facets of their being.

Murders and suicides

Murders and suicides are other scenarios that can result in souls becoming trapped. Those that have had their lives unexpectedly cut short by another's actions often get stuck with feelings of anger, revenge and sometimes confusion. They can become fixed in a situation in which they relive the final scenes over and over again. Such souls need a lot of love and support to help them let go and make their transition.

The same can be said of suicides, although from a slightly different standpoint. Most people who choose to take their own life do so because physical existence has become unbearable for them. We choose our own reality, and there is a cosmic principle that we are never confronted by more than we can endure. So any suicide can, at one level, be seen as a cop-out. However, some souls recognise that they have drifted so far from their intended karmic path that it makes no sense to remain in incarnation. Taking one's life, therefore, is seen as a quite legitimate option.

Each situation needs to be assessed individually, for there can be many different reasons why a soul chooses to take its own life. It is those spirits that commit suicide thinking they will escape reality which often get stuck. Once free of the body, such individuals often recognise that they have mistakenly curtailed their physical existence, but because of what has happened they are then unable to make the transition on their own. They will generally seek out friends they have known while alive and 'latch' on to them. If the friends are aware of this happening and know what to do, they can get help to allow these spirits to move on.

Capital punishment

No man has the right to take another's life, no matter how hideous the crime the other has perpetrated, and this applies equally to a state or country. What is permissible is the defence of one's own life or the freedoms we enjoy. Laws should allow complete freedom of expression as long as those freedoms do not cause suffering to others. Freedom of speech should be sacrosanct except where that freedom is used to incite violence, hatred or intolerance of others.

It is important that we defend our freedoms if these are threatened by those who would wish to see us enslaved. As one of my inner teachers once said, 'If you see a man wielding a stick and beating a child, then you need to take that stick away from the man.'

Sadly the sticks today can often be guns and, as recent events in Afghanistan have shown, it is sometimes necessary to take another's life to prevent some of the terrible abuses that individuals, through their own pain and suffering, wish to inflict on others. Nevertheless, when the stick has been removed and the individual restrained, then every possible step should be taken to help them rehabilitate themselves and regain a balanced state of living.

So what happens to the spirit that is executed through capital punishment? If humanity is lucky that soul will have realised the error of its ways and will make a rapid transition into the spirit world, where it will be helped with further healing on the spirit planes. This, sadly, is a rarity. More generally once such a spirit is out of the body and free it will use every opportunity to wreak further revenge on the society that put it through such misery. And how does it do this? Quite simply by seeking out other disaffected souls and encouraging them to further acts of brutality. A large element of the criminal fraternity comprises individuals who have been influenced or even possessed by spirits who seek to cause as much mayhem as they can. It is high time that unsocial behaviour was treated as an illness and not as a crime. Obviously individuals need to be restrained, but they should also be helped to realise why they have acted in the way they have; not uncommonly this stems from some abuse in their own childhood. If correctly treated, there are few individuals who would not respond to being helped to move beyond the need to commit crime.

I would urge any spiritual groups working in countries where capital punishment is still practised to do whatever they can to send thoughts of love, balance and release to those tormented souls who have to endure the termination of their own lives. If they can be sufficiently helped then there is hope that they will not return to further inflict the world with their desire for revenge. All thoughts of revenge on the part of the victims of their crimes are also counter-productive. As Christ so aptly put it, 'We reap what we sow.'

The innocence of children?

It is untrue to say that every baby is born innocent, for some spirits incarnate with deliberate intent to cause suffering to those around them. We only have to look at the lives of some of the dictators on the planet to see evidence for this statement. Yet in almost all these cases the flames of hatred have been further fuelled by their upbringing. There is a lot of truth in the adage 'Show me the child to the age of seven and I will show you the adult'.

Drug addiction and alcoholism

The last broad area that needs to be considered relates to those people who die from a habitual use of mind-altering drugs or alcohol abuse. I have already used music theory to provide an analogy for the way energy flows between people and within us, and once more this metaphor can come to our aid. What we put into ourselves in the form of food, beverages and any other substances holds vibrational frequencies, which influence the spiritual part of our being, while corresponding thoughts from our mind or spiritual self affect the body.

Are drugs a spiritual experience?

In the case of those who use drugs and alcohol, these substances, when taken into the body, provide a form of 'spiritual' experience; or perhaps a more accurate description would be to say that the spirit of the person undergoes, through resonance, a form of distorted spiritual experience when taking these substances.

In some traditions drugs are used to help open up a person to spiritual awareness, but for it to happen habitually or compulsively there has to be some part of the spirit that is self-destructive. The problems inflicted by this type of activity on the physical body are as nothing compared to the agony that occurs when a spirit leaves the body at death. It has become addicted to a form of experience that is body dependent, yet it no longer has a body through which to experience. Sadly many such spirits are not able to make the transition to the spiritual planes and become, in effect, Earth-bound.

I have helped a number of such spirits to move on, and in the process have become very conscious of the unimaginable suffering that they endure in this no-man's-land state. The only way they can get any respite is to attach themselves to another addict and obtain a form of secondary experience through their incarnate host. This only perpetuates the cycle, for the living addict is being further encouraged from the spirit world to maintain their addiction. This is one of the reasons why it is so hard for individuals to break free from a dependency on drugs or alcohol.

Those people who are involved with helping individuals in rehabilitation centres would do well to employ the services of a healer who can help these 'attached' souls make their transition. Failing this there is a very good chance that the addicted individual will fall back into their self-destructive ways.

Other cases

The above covers the majority of cases that I have tackled at different stages in my life. There are a few that fall outside these particular categories. Some cases have involved ritual sacrifices that date back in some instances to Druidic times. These have involved occult practices of a most unpleasant nature, and there is a considerable amount of negativity that needs to be dealt with before the spirits can be released.

These cases are all quite 'heavy' in that they deal with some of the deep traumas that we can experience. I would stress, however, that they are also a minority. The vast majority of people meet life's challenges before moving on to experience the realms of spirit without too much problem. As a healer you may come across the heavier types of case, and if you do it is as well to be prepared on how to tackle them.

I have helped a number of spirits in Egypt, trapped within their tombs, to make a full transition. Perhaps the most famous of these was the spirit of Tutankhamun.

The curse of Tutankhamun

I first became aware that Tutankhamun's spirit was still present within his tomb when I took a group of people to visit Egypt in the late 1980s. Until that time I had never given Tutankhamun much thought, but a number of the group, which included some psychic individuals, had a very negative reaction when they entered his tomb.

I checked this out by tuning into the tomb from a distance and was immediately aware that his spirit was still there. I later made enquiries of my inner teacher and was informed that this spirit was a very advanced, powerful soul, who had been murdered and then had become entrapped in the tomb with intense feelings of anger because of his anguish and hatred over what had happened to him.

We were advised not to try to exorcise his spirit as we would certainly not succeed and would only suffer a psychic kick-back. We were told that many people had tried unsuccessfully before to release this soul and had suffered in consequence. I wondered later whether this was the origin of the famous curse. We were encouraged just to send thoughts of love to his soul, which is what we did.

Over the next few years I had other opportunities to send helpful thoughts to this soul, particularly when visiting Egypt, but it was not until the Luxor massacre, when a group of tourists was gunned down in an area close to the Valley of the Kings, that I started to take the case of Tutankhamun more seriously. Ten days after this terrible event a small group of us had an opportunity to spend some time undisturbed in the tomb. It allowed us to communicate more directly with his spirit and to try to get him to let go of his desire for revenge and his wish to stay sealed in his tomb. It took two more years to complete this task, but after we invoked Tutankhamun's wife Ankensenaten and his father Akhenaten and sought their help we were finally able to release his spirit, and his tomb, I can now assure you, is free of his influence, which sadly, as far as Egypt was concerned, was far from benign.

These cases give a flavour of the type of situation that you might experience if you embark on trying to release trapped spirits or souls. In most instances this is a very easy, natural process, which can be undertaken with little fuss. Those few cases that are difficult need to be treated with considerable care. We will now consider the methods for releasing trapped souls.

Communicating with spirits

When you detect that a spirit is present you can communicate with it by sending either verbal messages or picture images. Your success will be dependent on your inner skills. You might be able to 'hear' through an inner voice what has happened to cause the spirit to become 'Earthbound' or 'see' what happened. It is not absolutely necessary to get a reply as you can still release the spirit (details will be given in the next chapter).

Preparation

The process of exorcism, as it is generally called (although I prefer to use the term soul or spirit release), is actually quite simple and need take only a few minutes to complete successfully. However, there are a number of very important stages in the process, which I will list in turn.

A Victorian ghost

Many years ago I was invited to the house of a young couple that my wife and I had got to know in Cheltenham. I knew they were interested in spiritual matters and held many views similar to our own. This was my first visit to their home, which was a small terraced cottage built at the end of the Victorian era, in a quiet cul-de-sac at the edge of the town.

Over a cup of tea they started to tell me about all the problems they had endured over the previous twelve months since moving into the house. As this was going on I suddenly became aware, in my mind, of a middle-aged man, with rolled-up shirtsleeves and braces, stomping up and down, in a real fury because people were invading his space. He was very upset, and doing everything in his power to get rid of the intruders. I could not help but mention this to the couple, who were very surprised, but the events they had experienced suddenly began to make sense.

Without more ado I said to them that I would release this soul and just needed a few minutes' quiet. As I have stated, the process is very easy and takes little time. So I closed my eyes, connected with this individual, informed him that he had passed over and suggested it would be better if he went to join his friends and relatives in the spirit world. I then opened up the portal and helped him through it. He left quite happy, so I reset the energy of the house and then opened my eyes.

The time lapse was probably no more than five minutes, at the very most, and could have been much less. What I had not anticipated was the effect on the couple. The man had an ashen face, for he had felt the temperature of the room drop to an icy cold as I was carrying out the clearing and had momentarily thought of fleeing in terror. Fortunately no harm was done, and since the clearing the problems in the house have disappeared. This experience taught me a lesson about letting house occupants know clearly what I am going to do, and now I generally prefer to work in a separate room unless there is a specific request from the occupiers that they be present.

Stage 1 – inner connections

You will need to spend as much time as you require establishing a connection with those spiritual beings that will help you with the clearing. In times past different cultures established their own modus operandi for the journey of a soul into the after-life. In Ancient Egypt this was fully described in what has been called *The Book of the Dead*, in which the most famous scene is the weighing of the heart on the scales of Truth in the halls of Osiris. The Buddhist lamas of Tibet have also encoded these steps in their Bardo. However, we do not need to worry too much about this process, for once the soul has made its transition there are many spirits who will then look after it. In *The Book of the Dead* it was the jackal-headed god Anubis who first led the soul on its journey, and this gives us a clue as to which archetype is most appropriate in facilitating the release.

In the Appendix you will find a chart showing the mythological connections that are manifestations of the eight primary spiritual qualities that are reflected at all levels on this planet (see p. 268). One of them is especially helpful in the transition between this plane and the next; the Ancient Egyptians knew this as the god Anubis.

Through long association with this energy, I have come to use another aspect of this archetype, which takes the form of a beautiful White Owl. I first made a connection with this particular symbol when I was working at a centre in the south of France in the early 1980s, and have described how people can connect with this symbol in my book *Develop Your Intuition and Psychic Powers.*[*]

It is very strange how ideas create ripples through life. Was it coincidence that inspired J. K. Rowling to use the very same symbol as Harry Potter's totem animal? I think not. I would like to suggest that the archetype of the White Owl is a living point of consciousness that everyone can call upon for help if they so choose. It is the energy I always invoke when carrying out exorcism work, and I know that it has helped numerous souls.

I have also introduced this symbol to many people who now work with it regularly to great benefit. It is very helpful in a wide range of activities, being able to point you in the right direction when you are undecided as to which path is correct. I would encourage you to carry out the following exercise, which will teach you how to connect with this energy, even if you think that you will never want to carry out an exorcism.

Connecting with the White Owl
Aim: To access an archetypal energy that will help with exorcism work and to discover an additional totem animal to help with protection
Time: 10–15 minutes

---

[*]Bloomsbury (1996).

Find a place where you can be quiet and will not be
disturbed and sit in your usual posture for meditation,
either on a chair or cross-legged on a cushion if you
prefer. During this exercise you will need to spend
time building up a connection with the symbol.

1. Close your eyes and make your usual connections
with your inner light and the Sun and the Earth. By
this stage these links should come quite quickly.

2. Now ask the Sun to send you the archetypal energy
of the White Owl and imagine that a magnificent
white owl is flying out of the Sun down a beam of
light to you. If you have connected in the right way I
can assure you that the owl will come. However, if
another animal manifests itself first, note what it is
and then connect with the Sun again and repeat your
request. You may need to ask three times before the
owl emerges, although in my experience it normally
comes at the first request.

3. When the owl arrives, allow your imagination to
sense where it is in relation to you. You might see it
in front of you, although in my case it first came and
sat on my left shoulder.

4. Start to communicate with this archetype as though
it were a real living being (which it is). You can begin
by sensing what you feel in your body, for example
the sensation in your fingers as you stroke its
feathers, or the feeling of its claws on your shoulder
or arm. What emotional feelings do you experience –
joy, maybe, or wonder? Can you hear the owl speaking to you in words when you ask it questions? If this
is difficult the owl will always communicate in a
visual way when you pose a question, by either
nodding or shaking its head depending on whether
the answer is 'yes' or 'no'.

5. You might like to ask the owl for its name. Harry Potter called his Hedwig. Just interpret whatever comes to you. Don't worry if you don't 'hear' a name. An image or symbol might come to you instead.

6. Now ask the owl to bring you another animal that can help by providing additional protection when you are carrying out any advanced healing work.

7. Link to the Sun again and see this additional animal coming down the beam of light to you. You will then need to repeat the process you used in connecting with the owl with this new animal.

8. When you have established these links they will always be open for you to access. Thank both of your animal guides and bring yourself back to full waking consciousness, but retain a sense of their presence with you.

The relevant exercises will need to be repeated regularly in order to build up a strong association with your animal helpers, the one you invoked as your power animal in Chapter 5 (see pp. 119–20), and now the White Owl and your additional protection animal. Once they are with you they will remain for as long as you need and use them.

In terms of protection I now have use of a 'lioness', which will quite happily sit quietly by my feet when everything is fine but gets up and starts to prowl around when there are negative energies around. This puts me on my guard.

Be on your guard – use your protections

The first step in any protection is knowing what you are letting yourself in for. Remember the adage 'Fools rush in where angels fear to tread'. There may be great wisdom in the fool, but in this instance I would strongly urge you not to carry out any exorcism or clearing work before checking with your White Owl that this is safe for you. Simply put the question to him (or her), and if the response is a shake of the head then go no further. There is no virtue in exposing yourself unnecessarily to danger. Exorcism is advanced work and should not be attempted unless you have had some experience in other types of healing, either through reiki or feng shui.

As your skills develop, so too will the ability to connect with different protective animals. For example, some people may find that their first protective animal is a deer or rabbit. Do not be put off if this occurs. Their protective strategy is to run away from danger, and if this is what is required then you need to heed their messages. This has nothing to do with cowardice; rather it is simple caution and prudence when embarking on an activity that does have its dangers if not approached in the right way. I would liken this to learning to drive a car; once the skill is mastered, and provided you obey the Highway Code, few problems will occur. Listen to the White Owl and he will never let you down. We should also remember that discernment is one of the very important spiritual lessons that we have to learn.

Different protective animals

Repeating the exercise used to connect with the White Owl will bring new animals when you are ready. However, do work with those that come and don't just reject them because they do not seem suitable.

Those who come from a Christian background might find the symbolism of the White Owl difficult, preferring to stay within the confines of their tradition. You can always call upon the Christ energy for help, but the archangelic presence that equates with the White Owl archetype is the archangel Cassiel. This is not a generally well-known angel, although the equivalent saint, St Christopher, is more widely recognised.

Most people call upon the archangel Michael for clearing work of this type but his/her energy is better suited to protection rather than help with the transition of souls. If you do not want to work with the White Owl concept, I suggest that invoking the presence of the archangel Raphael would be most appropriate for helping souls make their transition. Raphael is part of Judaic and Muslim tradition, so would be suitable for these faiths as well. As for Hindu believers, I would suggest that they call upon the elephant god Ganesa.

Stage 2 – commanding the spirits

Once you have created your inner links to your spiritual helpers, the next stage entails connecting with the spirit that needs releasing. In the vast majority of cases these spirits are lost and are only too willing to be helped; a few, through fear, will resist.

Is it appropriate to release a soul if they do not wish to go? Do we not have to respect their free will? But, equally, is it appropriate if, through their inability or reluctance to move on to the next plane, an imbalance is being caused in the energy matrix of a place? The answer is no. Spirits do need to move on. I would compare this with a five-year-old child going to school for the first time. As loving parents we need to take our children to school, as this is something they have to experience if they are going to progress. They might resist and play up, in which case gentle firm action and resolution are what is required. The same applies to any 'Earth-bound' spirit.

Developing the sensitivity required to be able to communicate fully with a spirit takes time. Do not expect that it will come overnight, although some people do acquire these skills very quickly. Remember that all communication is taking place within your mind. You will not actually see a ghost manifesting itself before you, so you do not need to worry. It is not necessary to get involved in a long dialogue with these souls. As has already been stated, they will get all the help they need once they get to the other side. Our task is simply to facilitate this transition.

You will need to command the spirit to come and stand before you. When carrying out your first exorcism, actually entering the room where the spirit is present is perhaps advisable, but with practice you can learn to command a spirit to come before you wherever they might be in the property. This has the advantage that sometimes you will become aware of spirits that were not at first apparent. In other words there might be more than one soul involved, although only one initially made its presence felt.

Symbol of the sword

The symbol I would recommend that you use to command a spirit is a sword, as this carries an energy of power and authority. This time, instead of the flaming sword, use the sword on its own, and point in turn to the four cardinal points of the compass, commanding, inwardly, in the name of the Father/Mother God, that all spirits come and stand before you. As long as this command has been made with sufficient belief and resolution, they will come. You do not have to voice this command unless you want to, for the thought itself carries sufficient power. Once they have presented themselves, you can then send them loving healing thoughts prior to releasing them. Remember that you are working for the highest good and for the best outcome for all.

Working in pairs

But let us suppose the spirits do not come or, even worse, choose to attack you. What can you do? It is for these reasons I always encourage people engaged in this type of activity to work in pairs. One of my hobbies is sub-aqua diving, in which venturing under water, which has potential dangers, is always carried out in 'buddy' pairs, in which it is your job to keep an eye on your 'buddy' and theirs to keep an eye on you. This is a very good principle to adopt if at all possible. In this case I would suggest that one of you keeps up a protection around the person who is doing the clearing.

I will go through these stages in greater detail when we come to the exercise; for now bear in mind that in principle any attacker will have to penetrate the protection of your partner to prevent itself from being released. This gives sufficient time for action to be taken to restrain your adversary, for this is what has to be done.

The golden net of Hephaestus

There is a symbol of restraint that I was taught many years ago, which has stood the test of time to good effect. In mythological terms this is called the net of Hephaestus.

Those of you who have read Greek mythology will know that Hephaestus was the lame smith god of the Olympians. He was the son of Zeus and Hera, and was skilled in making all sorts of magical implements. On one occasion, to catch out his wife Aphrodite (the goddess of love) in her liaison with Ares (the god of war), he created a golden net so fine that it could not be seen and so strong that it could not be broken.

Through this net Hephaestus was able to entrap the two lovers when they were cavorting in a bed and brought the gods of Olympus to witness what took place when his back was turned. It is a good story, and one that you might like to read for yourself. In principle you will need to throw this imaginary net over your assailant to restrain them, rather like a Roman gladiator.

In all my years using it I have never known this net
to fail once the spirit is trapped within it. As soon as you
have restrained the spirit you can then send your healing
thoughts in preparation for its release. At this stage any
aggression on the part of the spirit will have subsided, and
they will generally be open to receiving all the help they
can get. Both you and your partner can work together in
sending it healing.

Stage 3 – release

Once your spirit is restrained or standing quietly in front
of you, you can start the process of finally releasing them.
It is very important that this process is carried out
correctly – I have had to deal with a number of cases where
exorcisms have been performed by inexperienced people
in which the spirit has just been sent into a neighbour's
property. This might seem funny if you don't get on with
the neighbour, but it only causes more distress for the
'earth-bound' soul. Similarly I have been called in after
others have tried to help release souls and failed, often
ending up causing more chaos. If these steps are followed
correctly you will not fail.

All spirits who are trapped need healing and perhaps
also forgiveness. In essence this can be seen as a simple
thought of love which you send to the spirit, telling them
that everything will be well. Next you call on the archetype of the White Owl and the Sun, imagining that you are
bringing down a column of light around the spirit, which
links this physical realm to the next. As you gently lift
them into the light they depart with the White Owl to
guide them on their journey. I sometimes jokingly say that
I put them into a lift and press the button, which is, in
effect, what is happening.

When working with others I will always check that
they too sense that the spirit or spirits have departed,
but I have never known any failures in this respect. If you

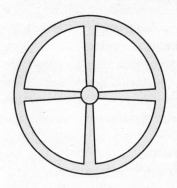

Fig. 10 Celtic or cosmic cross

feel any resistance, just call on the Sun and the White Owl for more help. They will not let you down. When the spirit has been released you will need to cleanse and rebalance the energies of the room, using the methods described in Chapter 7 (see pp. 154–62).

Finally, it is sensible to check that your own energy field is balanced, which you can do by getting your partner to send you healing energy and then doing the same for them. The easiest way to do this, if you have not participated in a healing course, is to place them on an imaginary white cross whose four points are linked by a surrounding circle (the Celtic or cosmic cross – see Figure 10). If you sense any negative energy, then mentally sweep through your auric field with your imagined flaming sword to cleanse and release what is stuck. Then inwardly thank your own spiritual helpers. Once the space is cleared in this way there should not be any more problems. What should you do if they do recur?

Problems

When chaotic psychic activity takes place in a property, or spirits keep returning, always look for a person as the cause. When this happens it can sometimes be very difficult to bring about a full healing, for you will need to tackle the reasons why a person is drawing these situations to themselves. This sometimes happens with children and can give rise to poltergeist phenomena.

There is a stage in adolescence when a child's sexual centres are being activated for the first time and sufficient energy is released for phenomena to occur. This is rare, and such problems usually arise when the child, often very psychic, has pent-up feelings of aggression towards its parents that it has never been able to express.

At one time I always thought that another spirit was involved in physical manifestations such as plates crashing to the floor, the spirit simply using the energies of the child. Now I am not so sure, for experience has shown that the child's own subconscious desires (its aggression) might also be a contributory factor.

It is this type of phenomenon which generally seems the scariest for people carrying our exorcisms. One simple tip is that manifestations can only occur when the psychic atmosphere is at a very heavy or dense level. Take the vibration up to a higher level by bringing imaginary sunlight down into the room and nothing of this nature will happen.

Possession?

Many years ago a woman came to see me claiming that she was possessed by a spirit that was trying to murder her. She described this offending presence as a hideous man dressed in black, whose oppressive emanations she could feel towering above her. Sitting down and tuning into this person, I could not sense any spirit presence, but just to be sure I cleared and sealed her aura. She continued to insist that the spirit was still there, so I asked inwardly for help and an inspirational thought popped into my head. I asked the woman directly, 'Who is it that you are trying to murder?' This question took her by surprise, but then with an anguished scream she collapsed in tears, sobbing that it was her husband from whom she had recently separated.

I never for one moment dreamt that she could have been capable of actually murdering her husband, but her anger and violent hatred towards him for what he had done to her were so intense that she could not accept these feelings as part of her nature. So she 'split' this aspect of herself off and denied its existence. The malefic force was part of her own self, come to haunt her.

In order to heal individuals who have psychic imbalances you will need to know a considerable amount about psychology and healing in general. There is not space in this book to cover all the different types of problem that can emerge in this context, but briefly these types of condition are often caused when individuals 'split' off part of their psyche because the offending part is too painful to accept.

During our many incarnations there will have been acts that we have committed about which we hold deep regrets. Sometimes these are so painful that we cannot accept them and they, in effect, become 'split-off' parts of the psyche, locked in time. There is a process called Soul Retrieval which seeks to tackle this problem, and I would suggest that anyone interested in looking deeper into this area should attend a course in this.

Here is the step-by-step exercise for releasing a trapped or Earth-bound spirit.

Releasing Earth-bound Spirits
Aim: To release a trapped or Earth-bound spirit
Time: 10–15 minutes

As has been stated, all clearing and releasing can be undertaken from a distance, but I would suggest that in the first instance you go to the property in question. You can carry out the work in the room where the presence has been detected, or any other room that seems suitable. I would also strongly recommend that you take a colleague to help you. You might also like to take a candle and perhaps some incense, although these are not absolutely necessary. I would suggest that before visiting the property you sit down, attune to the White Owl and ask whether you are ready to carry out this work.

Broadly speaking, when a case comes to us then we have reached a stage where we can begin working on this particular type of situation. Problems more often occur when we as individuals go looking for situations to tackle. But let assume that the White Owl has given his blessing, that it is safe to proceed and you are now in the room. (Before you enter, make sure that you put up your protections.)

1. Close your eyes and carry out the energy linking exercise given in Chapter 1 by connecting yourself symbolically with the Sun and the Earth. You might also like to invoke the help of the archangelic principles such as Michael and Raphael.

2. Call upon the energy of the White Owl and feel his presence.

3. Your colleague should now put up an additional protection around you using the protection exercise given in Chapter 2 (see p. 36). They also need to put a protection around themselves, but this should be secondary to their attention to you.

4. Imagine you have in your hand a sword. Pointing it in turn to the four cardinal points of the compass, command in the name of the Father/Mother God that the spirit present come and stand before you. If you are unsure that they have done so, then repeat this twice, making three times in all.

5. When you know that they are there, send your thoughts of love and healing to them, telling them in your mind that they will be fine and well looked after.

6. Then connect with the White Owl and the Sun and imagine that you are surrounding the spirit in a shaft of sunlight and very gently sense that they are rising up into the light and disappearing. You will know when they have gone.

7. Carry out the space clearing exercise given in Chapter 7 (see pp. 158–60), with you and your colleague working together.

8. Finally thank all those beings that have helped you and bring yourself back to full waking consciousness.

Note: Only if you sense that the spirit is being troublesome or tries to 'attack' you should you surround it in the 'golden net'. This will happen when you first command the spirit to come before you, so if you sense there may be a problem be prepared to act quickly.

If you have visited the property as a group with, say, four or five people, then so much the better, for you can then divide up the tasks, with some carrying out the clearing and others providing the protection. There are groups in existence which come together each month for 'rescue' work. In these cases they simply send out thoughts into the neighbourhood for any souls that are trapped or need help to move on to the next plane, requesting that they come into the centre of the group to be released. This is important healing work and can be of real benefit to the local community. The principle and methods given here can be adapted to suit your particular circumstances.

If you have been asked to carry out this type of work but have no colleague to assist you, then I would be very cautious. However, there is a symbol that you can link into for additional support if required. It is the symbol of a blue ankh in the centre of a blazing sun, superimposed upon a white cross whose four points are linked by a surrounding circle (see Figure 11). This triple symbol is connected with powerful spiritual energies that have been drawn down on to the physical plane. Use it whenever you need additional support and help.

Fig. 11 Symbol of ankh, Sun and cosmic cross

The need to release trapped souls

All imbalances affect the Earth at some level or another, and any spirit that is 'Earth-bound' or trapped is causing an imbalance. By releasing these souls you are helping the cleansing and rebalancing of the psychic and mental energy web of the planet. This is important work, and needs to be tackled by those who feel a calling in this direction.

Chapter 9

Earth Traumas and Other Imbalances

We now come to a whole range of more complex Earth energy disturbances. These are not easy to tackle and should only really be attempted if you are working within a group context. All subtle energy imbalances have their effect, and cleansing and clearing these disturbances helps us as well as the planet. It is important work, but does need to be approached with considerable care.

Negative site influences

These cover a wide range of disturbed subtle energies. How these energies affect you or your family is very much based on the individual. For some people even very negative energies appear to have little obvious effect. Others, however, can find a host of problems confronting them. These can include disturbed sleep patterns, seeing apparitions, health problems, out-of-character emotions (such as depression and anger), feelings of disquiet, and so on.

Black magic

Whether magic is white or black is basically a question of intention. If my intention is to heal and balance in a non-controlling way then that is 'white magic'. If I invoke forces to gain power and dominion over others then that is 'black magic'. It is as simple as that.

Disturbed energies that have been created by black magic rituals need to be approached with extreme caution. These are not easy to detect except by experience. However, if you find a very disturbed energy in a place, suspect that 'black' magic might be the cause. You can always use the symbolism of the White Owl to check by posing the question to the Owl and waiting for the reply. More importantly, consult your owl as to whether you can proceed safely to clear the problem or not.

It is important to appreciate that a desire to do good is not, in itself, enough. The basic principles of physics can be applied to these 'subtle' domains – quite simply, when two forces meet the stronger will always come out on top. If I were to step into a boxing ring with a professional fighter, all the good intentions in the world would not stop me getting a serious hiding. Much better not to enter the ring than to take on a situation where you know you will end up receiving a nasty black eye.

Black magic cases that use rituals, where forces are invoked to incite fear and gain power over others, can be current, in that the energies have been recently activated, or stem from some past period. In my experience black magic today is practised in quite a subtle way and seems to be aimed at ensnaring individuals into some group or cult, which the perpetrators use for gaining psychic and financial power.

The majority of cases that I have tackled involving places with distorted energy stemming from occult rituals reach back into Celtic times and sometimes beyond. The Celts certainly carried out human sacrifice in their rituals, and I have found instances of similar practices having taken place as recently as the seventeenth century, although strangely, perhaps, not in modern times. If ritual killing still goes on, then I believe it is quite rare, and does not happen to anything like the extent that some 'authorities' have suggested.

Clearing the negative energies of black magic cases

How to do this is not easy to describe, as each case will be different. You will need to free any trapped spirits and carry out the cleansing rituals already covered. But you may also have to tackle any negative spirit beings present, which will do everything in their power to stop you. And therein lies the danger. During my life I have had to tackle some very nasty demonic forces. They have to be caught, restrained, sent healing and love and then commanded to return whence they came. These battles take place in the mind and not in the way portrayed in some films – at least, that is my experience.

The one action that you can always take with complete safety, no matter what the situation, is to send a concentrated beam of love, like a laser of light, to the place or person. This has to be done through the heart. Love is the greatest protector and nothing will ever harm you if you just send love. It may not be as quick in dealing with the root causes of the problem, but it is 100 per cent safe. Even so, I would still urge you to work within a group context, with some members keeping up a protection.

Animal and human sacrifice

All rituals that involve sacrifice, whether human or animal, will draw fairly heavy dark influences, which then permeate the area. Spirits can easily become trapped by such practices, for reasons already given, and they endure considerable torment. I have also found that ritual killings or similar have been carried out under the cloak of the

Church, particularly during the Middle Ages, so there have been some very nasty activities perpetrated. These leave a considerable stain on the energy patterns of some places. Nor should we forget the terrible sufferings inflicted on those condemned of witchcraft, which in a strange way was also a form of ritual killing.

To cleanse these areas you will need to be able to invoke energy of the same magnitude as that used to establish this focus of negativity, and therein lies the potential problem, because it is very difficult to tell, before you actually begin, how much power you will need. If you have been able to fully harness the energy of one of the power centres mentioned in Chapter 3 then you will have considerable additional resources on which to draw.

Indeed, I would urge extreme caution in trying to tackle these types of case unless you have reached a level within a group where you can access the energies of a power centre. Even then you need to be able to work with symbols like the White Owl to forewarn you of danger and to observe the motto 'When in doubt, always pull out'.

Earth Traumas

Into this category comes a whole range of difficult Earth energies, including curses, battles, murders, massacres, and so on.

Lifting a curse

One of the very first clearings I participated in involved a curse laid against the London Opera Centre in the East End. To obtain the site some individuals had been dispossessed of their land and, in consequence, a curse was laid by one of them against the new property. A small group of us went to help break and clear this curse, which we successfully managed. This was the first time I experienced the feeling of extreme cold when entering a place with a disturbed energy. It is generally a sign that something is amiss.

Healing the energies of an old mental hospital

An acquaintance of mine purchased a property in a converted mental hospital that had been built in the middle of the nineteenth century. One of her rooms was always freezing cold, despite all her efforts to heat it. Mental hospitals attract all manner of psychic imbalance, and it was no wonder that she was experiencing problems. A number of traumatised spirits were present which had to be released; we then cleared the energy of the whole wing of which her property was part. Needless to say, after this was done the room returned to a normal temperature.

Curses

Curses can be laid against people as well as places. They are quite common in some cultures, particularly in Asia and Africa (voodoo), but not so common in Europe, although I have a Scottish acquaintance who tells me that cursing is quite common in Scotland. At one time she had inadvertently, in a moment of frustration and anger, cursed a plumber for not carrying out some work satisfactorily. When she rang to speak to him again, his wife said that he had just had an accident (about the same time as the curse was laid) and was now in hospital.

Bad luck

Many years ago I got to know an individual who had experienced an amazing run of bad luck. In most instances this is the result of one's karma, but on this particular occasion I became aware that someone had laid a curse against this individual, so in a quiet moment I carried out the necessary steps to lift the curse, which was successfully done. One of the manifestations of this particularly nasty disturbance was the inability of the person in question to sell his property, which had been on the market for about five years. Within three days of my lifting the curse he rang to let me know that he had received several offers for the property, one of which seemed very positive and, indeed, proved so, for the sale was finalised about six weeks later.

Curses can be quite difficult to detect unless you possess good psychic vision. Just because a person has a run of 'bad luck', do not assume that they have been cursed, for there are many other causes, such as your inner disposition (do you see your glass as half full or half empty?) or your personal karma. Equally, a curse should not be ruled out, and appropriate steps should be taken to lift it if one has been laid.

To lift a curse you will need to be able to wield a stronger energy than that wielded by the person who laid it. Whether you can or not you will discover either when you come to try to lift the curse or if you first ask the White Owl. So always ask first. You can use the symbol of the sword to cut any ties that are binding the person, and the negative force needs to be sent back to the perpetrator with a feeling of love and forgiveness.

Negative energy trails

Negative energy trails are caused by any form of human trauma that has occurred along a pathway. For example, such a trail might have been laid between a prison and a place of execution, or along a pathway used by refugees fleeing from a place of conflict. These trails can date back to the distant past, and will have an influence on any property through which they pass. To detect these types of problem you can use a variety of different methods, from listening to your feelings to using implements like a pendulum. To clear the energies use the space clearing technique described in Chapter 7 (see pp. 156–60). When a trail is detected, imagine that you are sweeping along the whole of the line so that everything is balanced, and not just the section that goes through your property or the property you are working on.

Plague line

On one occasion a close friend and I discovered that his house had been built on a pathway that had been used for carrying dead plague victims to a common burial site. This problem came to light when I stayed the night at his home and became aware of a very disturbed energy passing through the lounge, in which I was sleeping. It crossed under the stairs, where this friend had had a very serious accident when he fell from a stepladder, and out through the side of the house.

As we tuned into this line, my wife and I were very conscious of the connection with the plague and the suffering that had become woven into the Earth. When we relayed our discoveries to our friend he was quite amazed, and told us that his homoeopath had recently given him a remedy against bubonic plague without knowing quite why.

To corroborate our findings I asked a dowser friend to independently check out the site using a map of the house, without telling him what we had uncovered. He too discovered the same line running through the property in the same position, and described it as a 'black energy'. In cleansing this line we dealt with the whole track, and not just the part that went through our friend's home.

Battle sites

Battles leave great disturbances in the energy fields of the area where they have occurred, which need attention and healing work. There are so many sites that it is probably best for work to be carried out by groups living nearby. During the course of my life I have spent time working on a few battle sites, including Culloden in Scotland, which is close to a very important sacred site that holds the key to the balance of Scotland's energy. This proved to be one of the defining battles in the history of Scotland, which ended up creating enormous hardship for the common people.

William the Conqueror's invasion of England also brought with it some negative influences. I first became aware of this when carrying out some cleansing and energy rebalancing at a factory near Ilford, Essex. This was built upon an ancient sacred site that was part of a pattern of similar sites around London. I have no doubt in my mind that William fully understood the potency of ritual and the inherent power of place. His castles, like the White Tower of London, are positioned on too many sacred sites for this to be coincidence. From our inner perceptions we became aware of how he used rituals to break the pattern of previous energies in order to establish his own dominant force.

This accorded well with the story of William

performing a powerful ritual, using the bones of a Normandy saint, to change the prevailing wind when his fleet was prevented from sailing before the Conquest. Within three days, after many weeks' delay, the wind direction miraculously changed and the rest, as we know, is history. Over a period of time some colleagues and I tracked the different segments of this London ring in order to cleanse and rebalance its energies.

There are many other places around the globe where these types of imbalance have been created. Indeed, there is not a country in the world that has not at some time or another been subject to warfare and massacre; sadly, in some countries, these are still going on to this day. It is very important that the international community fully awakens to its responsibility for stopping the massacre of innocent people, using every method necessary, even measured force if required. The process of cleansing the Earth of all this negativity cannot really begin until we have stopped killing each other.

Generally it is not possible to clear all the negativity completely in one go. It is much better to see these sites as long-term projects, which should be tackled from time to time as deemed necessary. It is rather like stripping away the layers of an onion, reaching deeper and deeper into the core of the problem.

Ancient sacred sites

Ancient sacred sites like stone circles will have been used in many ways since the time they were first created. All these activities will have added their influence, and some of them may not be good. As has already been mentioned, human sacrifice was a part of Druidic practice, and some-times left very unsavoury energies in places.

Many old churches across Europe have been built on ancient sacred sites, and often these hold very beautiful energies that have been nurtured and handed down over millennia. Sadly, in a few cases the reverse is true. I have had to deal with a number of churches where black magic practices have taken place at different times in their history. Like attracts like, and if a church is built on a site that had previously been used for ritual sacrifice, the taint in the energy field of the place will often open the door to a similar occurrence at some later stage in its history.

Karmic influences

Karma is the law of 'cause and effect' applied over an extended period of time. With people, it is applicable over a number of incarnations. However, it is equally applicable to groups of individuals or countries and even planets.

People have a strange relationship with the power of place, for research has shown that genetic changes are more influenced by place than they are by race – the most obvious example are those caused by increased radiation levels. These influences may be more than just genetic. In other words, over a period of time people will start to act together in similar ways in accordance with some inherent pattern within a place. Why, for example, should Finland have a much higher incidence of suicide than, say, Sweden or Norway, which are similar cultures at approximately the same latitude? In some countries, such as the former Yugoslavia, we might question whether the tribal factions and infighting are part of the genetic make-up of the culture or whether some inherent dynamic within the land encourages this type of activity in its people.

Modern research into the genome is starting to provide some very fascinating insights into the migrations of human beings across the planet and the similarities between us all. According to Professor Bryan Sykes's book *The Seven Daughters of Eve*,[†] the entire current human

---

[†]Sykes, Bryan, *The Seven Daughters of Eve*, Bantam Press (2001).

population is descended from just one woman, the original 'Eve', who lived in Africa about 150,000 years ago. We are therefore all basically the same, and yet there are enormous differences in how some individuals and groups act. The terrible conflict between Israel and Palestine is a case of brother fighting brother, for there is practically no difference genetically between Jews and Arabs. So what other influences might be in play here?

Some of these we have touched on, for there is an undoubted tribal influence that is perpetuated when people act in a collective way. The spirits of those caught up in and perhaps killed in such conflicts will continue to influence their living relatives, perhaps inducing acts of aggression. It is a seemingly never-ending karmic wheel.

Yet if we dig a little deeper we find that there is also something inherent in the location which has encouraged this type of activity in the first place. It is strange, is it not, that the 'Promised Land' has witnessed such violence? Perhaps there was also a good reason why the Christ Spirit chose to incarnate in Palestine rather than any other country.

Before looking at what can be done to heal such situations, we need to dig a little deeper into their causes.

Destructive Earth patterns

It is sometimes thought that the moment of birth holds the potential of all that we are, which is why astrology, based on our birth charts, gives so many insights into our life patterns. Yet this is only part of the picture, for human beings principally derive their patterns both from their parents and from the spiritual consciousness that is the life force of their being – their spirit. It is therefore more correct to say that the moment of conception holds the potential for all that we are; at that moment both spiritual and somatic evolution are fused together in an amazing creative way, for it is at conception that the spirit first makes contact with the embryonic cell.

In the same way the conception and birth of a planet hold all the potential of its evolutionary development. At the moment of birth of our own planet certain waves of energy were moving through our solar system, which became infused into the matrix of the Earth. Held within these waves was a polarity between subservience and aggression. This is perhaps most obviously understood in human terms as the dynamic between victim and persecutor.

Aggression and subservience

We might therefore say that the 'genetic' pattern of the Earth encourages certain types of emotional response. The dynamic between aggression and subservience has manifested itself to a greater or lesser degree through all species that have evolved on this planet. It was reflected in the development of the dinosaurs and could be seen in the terrible ferocity of *Tyrannosaurus rex* as against the plant-eating passivity of the *Brontosaurus*. The reason that they, as a group, disappeared was because they had reached a point in their evolution when they were collectively stuck. They no longer provided a mechanism for the resolution of this imbalance, so Gaia/Geb engineered their extinction through a comet impact.

One of the deeper karmic reasons for human development on this planet has been to work through these two extremes in order to find a balance, which will then provide a form of integration between these polarities which the Earth has, so far, not been able to achieve. This extremism is also reflected in the balance, or rather imbalance, between the masculine and feminine elements of our nature. By integrating these dynamics within ourselves we are positively helping the balance of the Earth.

In order to do this human beings have had to

collectively experience these twin forces in all their destructiveness, and will continue to do so until we can really integrate these energies. We stand on the threshold of a new epoch when the need for war and aggression will cease. When this happens the effect on the collective dynamic of this planet will be enormous. Before the final integration is achieved pockets of conflagration will continue to erupt with considerable violence, which is what we have witnessed and are witnessing at the moment.

Healing must start with us

There are a number of ways in which the integration of these energies can be tackled. First and foremost we each need to begin to balance the dynamic between anger and acquiescence within us. This cannot be done by denying that both of these states are an integral part of our being. You cannot deal with your aggression by running away from it. Only by fully integrating these polarities will a balance be achieved, for at that point we will no longer be helplessly driven by either of these two forces but will be able to freely choose between them.

This is not easy, for it requires complete honesty and openness. The person who rejects their potential for anger will only succeed in drawing angry or violent people to them, for balance needs to be found. In order to bring peace to this planet, tempered aggression will be required for some time to come in certain circumstances, but fundamentally the only way peace will be found is through dialogue. This is why it is important to look at ourselves without being self-critical or judgemental.

The recognition that your enemy is only a reflection of you is the important shift in perception that needs to be made. There is a balance that has to be struck. This is why, when applied to the planet, needless destruction becomes self-destruction. Imbalances being caused to the weather

through pollution are going to reap some terrible consequences for humanity.

Healing the karmic patterns of the Earth

Because these patterns are woven into the Earth itself we
can also send thoughts of balance to the planet, focused
on those areas where aggression predominates. In these
cases it is not appropriate just to send *light*, for very
often all this does is simply invoke the *shadow*. The most
appropriate symbol to use in these cases is the weaving
of yin/yang energies found in the Tao (see Figure 12).

You will need to visualise this symbol holding all the
extremes in complete balance and harmony; then project
the symbol into the land with a strong thought that it is
providing integration and balance to the Earth itself.

Fig. 12 The balance of the Tao

You might like to
imagine that this balance
is extending right down
through the upper atmos-
phere, to the crust of the
planet and then on into
its fiery core. I would
then project an additional
symbol of the ankh, Sun
and cosmic cross (see
Figure 11, p. 194) into
the land, bringing a
further quality of healing
and balance. This type of healing work can be safely
carried out regardless of what is taking place 'energetically'
in the region. It might seem presumptuous to consider
that the Earth needs healing, yet, as I have stated, there are
aspects that are out of balance and need correction.

At this moment this aggressive quality is being
further fuelled by those Luciferic forces that want to
encourage fear and hatred on this planet, for this is their

source of sustenance and power. To clear and cleanse the influence from these negatively polarised beings requires a considerable degree of insight and is best not tackled directly. Rather aim to encourage a feeling of balance and love within the leaders of those groups that so easily slide into violence.

Murry Hope, in her book *The Gaia Dialogues*, makes a very similar claim. She calls this wave of extremism a virus. Looking into the future, to a time when this imbalance will finally be corrected, she states: '... the lion will indeed lie with the lamb, for the world-wide aggression which has formed such an integral part of the viral symptoms will slowly recede. Different species will no longer need to kill each other in order to survive and mankind will, at last, come to understand and respect the life-force in all things.'

To heal disturbances caused by karmic imbalances, use the exercise at the end of this chapter.

Cleansing and healing

For all the reasons already given, the cleansing and balancing of the vibrations of a place with severely disturbed energy need to be tackled with considerable caution.

Although I see no reason to needlessly put myself in danger, and I always tread very warily, I have had my fair share of scrapes. These have occurred when I have not taken sufficient preparatory steps, or have made assumptions without fully checking out the problem. I very rarely work on my own in such circumstances, for the group dynamic is very important.

If you wish to help, then sending thoughts of love to a place will always be of benefit; the more these are focused and directed at different situations on the planet, the easier will be the Earth changes that we are all beginning to witness at the moment. The following exercise can be safely used to help this process.

Cleansing a Site with Disturbed Energies
Aim: *To cleanse an area with disturbed energy*
Time: 15–20 minutes

This exercise should only be carried out within a group context. If you can meet in a room that is used just for healing purposes, then so much the better. Sit in a circle and include within it representations of all the four elements. A candle is suitable for fire, a crystal for earth, a bunch of flowers or perhaps a feather can represent air, and a bowl of water the final element. I would recommend that one person act as master of ceremonies by getting the group to focus together at the different stages. I would also urge that some of the group focus solely on keeping up the protections.

1. Each person should attune, carry out the linking exercise to the Sun and the Earth and put up their protections.

2. Next carry out the group harmonisation exercise given earlier in this chapter.

3. You now need to call, in turn, upon the energies of the four elements, asking them to enter your circle and support you in your healing work.

4. Next make any suitable connections with other spiritual beings – the ascended masters, archangels, and so on, depending upon your own belief structures.

5. If you have made a connection with a spiritual power centre, then open up this link and feel the energy flowing around your group.

6. Spend time really feeling the harmony and love between you.

7. Those who are working on the protection should focus on maintaining a balance in the energy fields.

8. The other members of the group can imagine that the area or place that needs to be cleansed is in the centre of the room. Using first the symbol of the Tao and then the Aquarian cross, project these on to the site, sensing that they are bringing healing and balance, releasing any negativity that is present.

9. Imagine that all disturbed energies are being funnelled up through the centre of the room and out into the sunlight, where they are transformed and balanced. Allow a feeling of love to flood the site, adding to the transformational process. These last two steps need take no more than two or three minutes. Far better a short, concentrated beam of balancing energy than ten minutes of drift, during which the mind wanders.

10. Finally lift the image of the place into the sunshine and re-establish the balance and harmony within the room.

11. The energies opened up now need to be closed down. First close the link with any power centres you are using, then dismiss the four elements, thanking them for their help, and likewise any other spirit influences you have invoked.

12. All participants should bring themselves back to full waking consciousness. You can now discuss what you have experienced.

If you wish to tackle more than one case, that is fine, but I would not recommend that you take on more than four cases at a time as this work is tiring. If you do two or more cases, instead of each half of the group in turn sending healing to a specific place you could work it so that one half sends healing to Palestine and in the next case the other half sends healing to, say, Afghanistan. In this way everyone gets to practise sending healing and keeping up a protection.

You can adjust this modus operandi to suit the conditions of your particular group. Don't forget the Chinese saying: 'From small beginnings great things can be achieved.'

Chapter 10

Geopathic Stress and Electromagnetic Pollution

We now come to two areas which, it is claimed, are currently causing a lot of problems, most of them unrecognised but potentially generating a variety of ailments such as tiredness, inattention and headaches. The term electromagnetic pollution gives immediate clues as to the nature of this new, unseen invasion of our energy fields. Geopathic stress is less familiar to the general public and is certainly more difficult to define. So let us start with this topic.

Geopathic stress

Geopathic comes from two Greek words, *geo*, meaning 'of the Earth', and *pathos*, meaning 'suffering' or 'disease', so literally we could define the term as 'the stress generated from the suffering or diseased Earth'. Into this category come a whole host of problems, which dowsers and those practising kinesiology (muscle testing) have started to detect over the past 20 years or so.

Kinesiologists show that certain muscle groups test strong or weak when exposed to different substances or energy patterns. This system is used widely to test for food intolerances, but also for any other type of potential energy imbalance. Practitioners have been able to show that certain places can and do cause a weakening in specific muscle groups when individuals stand on or close to them.

Something within the environment is having a negative influence on the individual in question, and the claim is often made that this can eventually lead to serious health problems if a person is over-exposed to such an influence through, for example, sleeping in such a place. Such claims are hard to prove scientifically, and I am not aware of any proper studies having been carried out in this field, but anecdotally there certainly appears to be an element of truth in these assertions.

My own explorations into this field are somewhat bizarre because I have never been aware of 'geopathic stress' in quite the way it is interpreted by various acquaintances and health practioners I have met. Undoubtedly there are energies that come from the Earth or surround the Earth which give problems, but generally these seem to me to have a specific cause, such as in the case of the plague line mentioned in Chapter 9. I cannot recall whether the dowser who plotted the 'black line' through the property mentioned the term geopathic stress, although he may well have done. It may be, therefore, that dowsers and kinesiologists are lumping together a whole host of different imbalances under one catch-all title; certainly, when reading Jane Thurnell-Read's informative book *Geopathic Stress*,[‡] this is the feeling I get. We might therefore say that 'geopathic stress' is either:

- Our response to a natural physical or subtle earth energy pattern which in itself may be neither good nor bad. For example, we normally consider the Sun's rays beneficial, but if I were to stand out in

---

[‡]Thurnell-Read, Jane, *Geopathic Stress*, Element (1995).

the blazing sun for any length of time I would get
sunburnt, while a native African would not have the
same problem. In a similar way there may be
natural energy within the Earth, such as underground streams, which affects some people but not
others.

• A subtle energy that has originated from some form
of negative human activity.

We do need to be clear about whether the distorting
energy in question relates to the electromagnetic spectrum
or whether it is an aspect of subtle energy. When we come
to look at electromagnetic pollution, such as the overuse
of mobile phones, we can be sure that these are part of the
physical world. However, many phenomena claimed
under the title geopathic stress may not be physical at all.

Below ground or above ground

Another way in which these distorting energies have
sometimes been classified is based on whether their
origins lie within the Earth, which basically covers all
aspects of geopathic stress, or whether they are in the
'atmosphere' of a place or above the Earth, such as occurs
with ley lines or when Earth-bound spirits are present.

The difficulty I have with this type of classification is
that there is often an overlap between the two, and the
causes of distortion in the energy fields may have very
similar origins, the principal difference being the time span
between when the event happened and the present day. Over
time archaeological evidence gets buried deeper and deeper
below the surface. The same happens to energies. For
example, the feelings of grief and anguish emanating from
the plague line were both within the earth and above it.

The case of a site that I worked on in Cornwall called
St Nectan's Glen offers an example of the complexity of
this type of phenomenon.

St Nectan's Glen (part 1)

In my early twenties I visited a beautiful waterfall in Cornwall called St Nectan's Glen, in which resides a very powerful devic water being. Communicating with this being was and is a very wonderful and deeply meaningful experience, which always leaves me with a beautiful feeling of peace. At the top of the waterfall is a small bungalow and a café, adjoining which is an outbuilding on the site of the original hermitage of St Nectan, after whom the valley was named. Since that first visit this place has always attracted me whenever I am in Cornwall, as it lies near Tintagel and many other especially sacred sites in the area.

A few years after this first visit I happened to hear from some friends of mine that the property and valley had come on to the market, and they were interested in purchasing the place. However, they had carried out some research and found that since the bungalow had been built in the early 1900s there had been a number of challenging problems. All the occupants had experienced difficulties on an emotional and psychological level, such as the break-up of a marriage, mental breakdown, and so on. This was clearly a house with a lot of problems. I have been unable to verify independently whether these accounts are true, as stated, but it seemed to me that the likely cause was the presence of this powerful devic spirit in the waterfall and the proximity of the water, which had caused an imbalance within the occupants of the property.

Why is it that we are affected by some natural Earth energies? The reasons can be many and varied, but one is to do with our inner balances.

Balancing the four elements within

Human beings are composed of all four elements – earth, air, fire and water. This fourfold nature can been seen at all levels with us. For example, earth relates to the physical body, water to the emotions, air to the mind, while fire symbolises our spirit. This is why it can be useful to light a candle when meditating. The candle symbolises the fire element, relating to the spiritual aspect of our being.

Yet each layer of our self – our physical body, emotions, thoughts and our spiritual self – can also be further subdivided in terms of this fourfold nature. For example, anger is a fiery expression of the emotions, while sadness or melancholy is a more earthy emotion, and so on. Each plane within us carries the fourfold imprint of these patterns.

Each person is unique, and each will have his or her elemental preferences, so some will relate to the element of 'fire' in preference to, say, 'earth'. These predilections are sometimes picked up in astrology from the sun sign or ascendant, but these should not be taken for granted because other factors are involved from our genetic inheritance to the desires of our spirit.

These preferences have been noted in the business world with managerial assessments such as the Myers Briggs test which demonstrate that there are basically four types of manager, and a well-run company needs individuals who exemplify each of these types for balance to occur. If a company has no 'practical' (earth) person or manager they might have wonderful ideas (fire) but never meet the deadlines, and so on. Water-type managers deal with the feelings of well-being within a company – the human resources manager – while air types deal with communication – the marketing manager.

Unlucky gems

When we as individuals come into contact with one or other element in the natural world, it can tend to exaggerate that corresponding component part of us. If overdone this can have the effect of pulling us out of balance.

Some of the famous precious stones in the world, like the Hope diamond, often have stories attached to them to the effect that they bring bad luck to their owners. Such stones have very powerful Earth elemental spirits within them, and it is this which causes the problem – not because there is anything intrinsically wrong with the gem, but because the owners cannot handle its energy. When this happens they get pulled out of balance and then health or emotional problems can occur. Remember the example of me standing out in the sun.

In recent times individuals have become very attracted to crystals, and I have known people who have started to acquire large numbers of these semi-precious stones.

I have already discussed how crystals can often carry the trauma of the place where they are mined, but at another level the exposure to many crystals can, in itself, cause imbalance, and I have seen this happen to a number of people. These imbalances have manifested themselves in different ways – health or financial problems, even the break-up of relationships. It all depends on whether you can handle the energy or not, and how you balance this with the other three elements. As human beings we need continually to strive for balance between each of the elemental principles; if we start to explore one or other element deeply it is important to try to balance this in other areas of our lives.

St Nectan's Glen (part 2)

It seemed to me that the problem was to do with the fact that the occupants of the bungalow were exposing themselves to flowing water that ran alongside their property before tumbling down from a considerable height as a magnificent cascade. Over-exposure to water and the energy of the powerful devic being were certainly contributory factors in causing problems for the occupants of this place. My friends decided not to go ahead with the acquisition. It was bought by another purchaser, who continued to allow people access to the waterfall.

I visited the valley several times after this, but there was a gap in the early 1990s. The next time I turned up was at the end of a weekend's pilgrimage to Cornwall, during which a small group of us had visited a number of sacred sites in the area, including some very special places on Bodmin Moor. We had just visited Tintagel, and felt that we could not leave the area without going to St Nectan's Glen, which we did.

Access is via a beautiful walk through woods along-side a bubbling stream. Arriving at the bungalow, expecting to find the usual welcome, we were very surprised to discover access closed. I knocked on the door and was answered by the owner, who informed me that he had closed off access to the waterfall the previous year after a series of very aggressive confrontations with members of the public. We explained our mission, and he very kindly allowed us access to the fall. From what he had told us it was clear that some other serious energetic imbalance was causing the problems, beyond just the presence of this beautiful deva. So we carried out some healing work, cleansing the site and releasing a spirit that was trapped either in or close to the bungalow. There were also some energy imbalances that dated back to the time of St Nectan himself. We also created a mental shield around the property to insulate the occupants from the impact of the devic spirit.

I visited the site again in September 2000 and the transformation could not have been more startling. The café was open again and my partner and I were greeted with a very warm welcome. It appeared that the owner had opened up the property again soon after we had carried out the cleansing and healing work. He had cleared out the original hermit's cell, which had been full of rubbish, and turned it into a meditation room. The waterfall has now become a shrine, with many prayer stones and Celtic prayer ribbons adorning the trees. It is a truly startling transformation, which delights my heart, and if you get the chance it is a wonderful place to visit. Nor, to my knowledge, have there been any more problems with members of the public.

The reason for telling the St Nectan's Glen story at length is to highlight the complexity of the different strands, woven one on top of another, each of which contributed to imbalance, at some level. Underground streams, when they flow under buildings, are often viewed as potential problem areas, and it is generally recommended that one should not locate one's bed over such a stream. In most cases these are detected through dowsing, and checking your property for patterns and disturbed energies can be useful. However, if you are an individual with a natural empathy for water, then I would suggest that you would have no problem with underground water, in which case a kinesiology test may be the most appropriate way to check your responses within the house. Yet in the situation of the bungalow at St Nectan's Glen there were clearly other factors involved. The property needed clearing and an 'earth-bound' spirit had to be released, so steps may be required to clear disturbances above ground as well.

Black streams, underground springs

Underground water generates an influence that can certainly be detected by dowsers. When two streams cross a vortex is created which can be picked up not only through dowsing but also through muscle testing, where a weakening in the muscle strength can be observed.

What is strange about these energy vortices is that they are also found under megalithic standing stones. This has led some people to suggest that the Neolithic and Bronze Age peoples detected these stream crossing points and deliberately erected standing stones to mark their position.

However, more recent researches have found that simply putting up a standing stone in a neutral place appears to attract water to it, causing a detectable crossing point of energy. In this, then, we have a classic chicken-and-egg situation. Did the energy vortex come first or does the stone in some way create the vortex? Perhaps the very intention of placing a stone at a particular site causes the anomaly – thought impacting on matter. This type of situation is quite complex.

Another claimed underground disturbance comes from energies called 'black streams'. These are said to be underground water channels that have become blocked or polluted with negative energies. A German dowser and researcher, Baron von Pohl, developed a scale from 1 to 16 to classify the negative effects of these streams. Anything above 4 on this black-stream Richter scale caused physical health imbalances, including cancer, cot deaths and arthritis. He went on to claim that almost all known diseases are caused by over-exposure to these energies.

To my mind this is a great over-simplification, for all the reasons already given. Health is not just dependent on where we live but on a whole host of factors, not least of which is the food we eat.

Black streams and similar underground negative influences are normally corrected by dowsers by placing copper rods or copper springs into the ground at appropriate places, thereby diverting the stream or transforming its energy into a beneficial influence.

Elemental imbalance

In some cases the elemental forces themselves can be out of balance, which reflects back, in an adverse way, on the inhabitants of a property. Many years ago I came across the case of a spiritual centre in the Cotswolds where negative feelings in the atmosphere were traced to quarrying being carried out many miles distant. The effects of blasting the stone created problems, particularly for the Earth elemental beings, which manifested themselves in the valley where this centre was located. Sending healing to the quarry brought a dramatic change in the energy of the place.

I suspect that the elemental forces themselves sometimes 'play' with those carrying out healing work, for I have come across several instances where the negative energy has just moved a few feet to one side or another once the coils have been inserted. Whether this type of approach is successful or not depends very much on the operator and how in tune they are with the elemental beings that lie behind this type of disturbance.

Personally I have never bothered to work with copper coils or anything similar as I consider it unnecessary. Communicate with the elemental presences (ask whether they are happy or not, and if not why not) then carry out the exercise given on p. 224 and the problems will be corrected.

Detecting geopathic stress

From what has been covered so far you will appreciate that there are many levels to this subject. Geopathic stress is normally detected through dowsing or through muscle testing. However, as far as I am concerned all this tells us is that there is some energy imbalance within a place that needs correction. As a matter of principle it is always helpful to balance the energies of your home or place of work, which I suggest should be done regardless of what might or might not be there. If you follow the procedure given here you will not go far wrong and will certainly correct most problems, the only limitation being the power of your thought and intention.

Working with the spirits of the elements

When confronted by a situation where I suspect elemental involvement, which includes many aspects grouped under the heading of 'geopathic stress', I will always contact the elemental beings to ascertain the cause of the problem. It may be that in the past, when the house was being built, say, some important area, from their perspective, was upset or disturbed. So sending them thoughts of love, asking for forgiveness, is always appropriate. Above all they want and need to be acknowledged, and the more you can open up to their realms the better. Such awareness does take time and practice but the perseverance is worth the effort.

We are all unique individuals and will respond to elemental forces in our own individual way. It is generally a case of one man's meat is another man's poison. Should you move into a property where there is a powerful elemental presence, such as an underground stream, then you may need to take steps to counter this, not because there is anything wrong with the stream but because it may have an adverse effect on you. The simplest way to deal with this is to put a balancing barrier between you and the energy. The following exercise will show you how.

Protection from Geopathic Stress or Other Earth Energies

Aim: To create a barrier against any energy that emanates from the Earth which causes you a disturbance in your own energy fields

Time: 10–15 minutes

Find a place in your home where you can be quiet and will not be disturbed and sit in a chair with your feet on the floor.

1. Close your eyes and carry out the linking exercise to the Sun and the Earth given in Chapter 1 (see p. 18).

2. Connect in your mind with the energies within the Earth under your home and try to sense how they feel. If there is a perception that something is not right, connect to both the Sun and to the 'heart' of the Earth and, drawing upon this energy, send it into the Earth under your home with the thought that it is healing and balancing any disturbances. Do ask the elementals for their forgiveness on behalf of humanity if anything has been done that has upset or disturbed that part of their realm where your property stands.

3. When you have completed this stage, imagine that you are placing a large white Celtic cross (a white cross with arms of equal length within a circle) under your house with the thought that any energy coming from the Earth will only pass though the cross in a balanced way not harmful to you or your family members.

4. Finish by thanking the elementals for their help and bring yourself back to full waking consciousness.

This exercise can be done just once, as for clearing and setting the energy within your home (see pp. 158–60), or more often if you suspect that there is a deeper level to any problem. As your experience grows, so you will be able to effect changes at more profound levels.

I have always found the Celtic cross symbol (or cosmic cross, as it is sometimes called) to be effective in dealing with any disturbances from the Earth, although I will always seek out and try to clear the root origin of any problem first.

We can only do what we are capable of doing at any one time. If you suspect a problem but do not have the confidence to tackle it there and then, the above steps will alleviate any negative effects. I would then recommend that you seek out expert advice to complete the task.

Ley lines

We have already touched on this subject, but these energies can also be a problem for some people. To be clear about what was previously said, I would define ley lines in three ways:

1. Imaginary trackways linking ancient sacred sites, such as stone circles, standing stones, mounds, medieval churches, and so on (Watkins's original definition).

2. Lines of energy linking two or more power centres together. In this definition there may be an overlap with sites in the first definition. For example, there may be a connection between two stone circles if this

was deliberately set up in the past, by linking energies together to create a matrix. We might call these
power lines.

3. Thought lines generated when people communicate
together on a telepathic level.

I would also stress again that ley lines, as defined in 2 and
3 above, have nothing to do with electromagnetic energies. They exist solely on a subtle energy level and run
overground, rather than being within the Earth.

In most instances few people would be bothered by
the first and third definitions; it is the second that can
cause problems. If a powerful ley line linking two major
sacred sites passes through a property then the occupants
can be energetically disturbed, as described earlier in this
chapter and in Chapter 3. The strong subtle energy can
upset some people's energy balances, leading to a variety
of problems. If you suspect that this might be a problem,
check the alignment of the power line, through what you
sense within or through dowsing, and then see whether it
links to any sacred sites in your area. Then follow the
procedure given below.

Golden pyramid shielding device

A shielding device is the appropriate mechanism for
coping with this energy. Some individuals place copper
rods in the ground. My own solution is much simpler. I
create in my mind an imaginary golden pyramid with a
solid golden base, which I see fully encompassing the
property, and then visualise the ley line energy passing
around the place rather than through it. I also carry
out any necessary clearing and rebalancing within the
building and reset the atmosphere as already described on
pp. 158–60. Finally I send healing thoughts of balance to
the occupants just for good measure.

Sha lines

The final Earth energy force that deserves a mention is Sha lines. The concept of Sha lines stems from the principles of feng shui and the natural balanced energy called Ch'i. Nature does not normally create straight lines, and for this reason feng shui proponents assert that straight alignments generate destructive energies called Sha lines. When balancing the energies of a place, they will always do what they can to create blockages in alignments, so that the energy flows around objects, rather like a river meandering across a plain.

Despite having a high regard for the principles of feng shui, I see this as a mental construct that has no real basis in landscape energy terms. The principle of finding harmony with the land is totally valid, but to project this further and state that alignments create problems is not. Most of the modern capitals of the world incorporate alignments in their street plans, and these do not per se cause any energy imbalances. If we love the Earth and all that it contains we can build as many alignments as we choose without suffering any ill consequences.

Summary

To deal with these types of problem you will need to determine whether the subtle energy comes from within the Earth (geopathic stress) or above the Earth (ley lines). You can do this quite simply by asking your White Owl, by dowsing, or by using the image of the traffic lights – whichever you prefer. Do, however, make the inner connections to the Sun and Earth first as described in Chapter 1, p. 18.

To correct any imbalances, use a *Celtic cross* for any problems that stem from within the Earth; use a *golden pyramid* for those problems that flow above the Earth. In all cases communicate with the elemental forces of the area and get their help wherever you can. If these steps are followed the majority of those cases which fall into the category of geopathic stress can be satisfactorily tackled.

Electromagnetic pollution

We now come to an area that quite definitely comes within the realm of physicality. In recent years human beings have started to expose themselves to a vast range of electrical frequencies far in excess of what we have experienced before. These most certainly do have an effect on the body, but whether or not this effect is harmful to us is another issue.

We need to be absolutely clear that electromagnetic energy is a natural phenomenon on this Earth. It is an expression of the elemental forces of the planet, which are not affected by these energies in any way. Even within a nuclear reactor or in the detonation of a hydrogen bomb the elemental forces operate quite happily. If we are upset by these energies – which might happen if, for example, we over-expose ourselves to radiation from radioactive substances – this is just another case of standing out in the blazing sun. If we get burnt then this is our problem, not theirs.

A modern phenomenon

I first came across a problem caused by electromagnetism when I heard a lecturer describe the difficulties his wife experienced when she stood within the electrical fields generated by the ring main in her house. She suffered from a whole series of health problems which, although not seemingly serious, as the doctors could find no obvious cause, nevertheless proved to be very debilitating, resulting in a form of myalgic encephalomyelitis (ME). I cannot recall how it was discovered that electricity was causing her problems, but as soon as steps were taken to shield her from these influences the symptoms vanished. Some of the measures she had to adopt were quite bizarre, including using aluminium foil in a hat which she had to wear whenever she was inside the property.

In the modern world we expose ourselves to a wide range of electrical frequencies, through televisions, power cables, computers and, more recently, mobile phones. All this is very new to human beings, and the long-term consequences cannot at this stage be determined. Our bodies are held together by electromagnetic energy fields, and in exposing ourselves to these outside energies we are certainly causing changes within us. Whether this is a problem for you or not again comes back to your individual make-up. Some people may be more seriously affected than others. In principle the more balanced we are the fewer problems we will experience.

Testing devices

Since coming across the potential problems caused by electricity I have acquired a very sophisticated item of equipment for testing the electromagnetic energy fields of the body called the BioMeridian Stress Assessment system. This works by testing the balance of the acupuncture points on the fingers and feet.

The discovery of the link between the acupuncture points and the electromagnetic energy fields of the body is a fascinating story, showing the link between the physical energies of the body and the subtle energy fields known to the Chinese as Ch'i. It stemmed from the pioneering work of a German doctor called Rheinhold Voll, who researched these links in the 1950s and 1960s. Since then many devices have been created based on his research which can be used to assess health balance as well as test for food intolerances and a range of disease-causing problems. Into this category comes electromagnetic pollution.

The impact of electromagnetic pollution

Using this equipment, it is very easy to detect whether an individual is affected by different types of electro-magnetic influence, including mobile phones. There is no doubt in my mind that all these devices are having an effect, but certainly some people are better placed than others to counter these negative influences.

In recent years I have made regular visits to Finland, the home of Nokia and the mobile phone, and have been concerned about the number of people I have tested for health balances who have been caused problems by this form of disturbance. It is hard to say whether this will have long-term consequences for their health. It is also true that those who come to see me for treatment are people who already have some health problem, at least in the majority of cases, so the sampling might already be biased.

In broad terms, based on the results from my testing equipment, I would say that the following devices are likely to cause some imbalance in your energy field.

- Mobile phones
- Computers
- Televisions
- Mains electric cables
- Overground power pylons
- Microwave cookers
- Global positioning system (GPS) navigators

Protective devices

The most obvious protective step you can take is to try wherever possible to cut down on your exposure to these energies. For example, laptop computers emit less radia-tion than conventional computers. Sit at least six feet away from a television (although it is very difficult to get young children to do this). Switch off electrical supplies whenever possible.

There are also shielding devices on the market which can help us rebalance our energies. It would appear that these devices operate not by shielding the user from the offending microwaves (in the case of mobile phones) but by realigning the body's own energy fields. At least, this is true of those devices I have tested using my equipment. Indeed, I can rebalance the energies of the body using my equipment, and the effects appear to last for some considerable time, depending on the individual and the particular level of exposure. Some of my clients, who were previously seriously affected by computers, are now rarely bothered by their use. If our energies are in balance, then we are resistant to most problems.

This is a potentially very contentious area, for the freedom of communication offered by mobile phones is enormous, but we do need to be cautious, and there is no doubt in my mind that some individuals are quite badly affected by electromagnetic energies. One of the causes is a weakness in their 'etheric energy field', which I can test. If you are affected in this way, you can consciously strengthen your field by imagining that you are putting on a silver suit under your clothes. This will strengthen your etheric energy field and help it to shield you from the 'negative' influence of electromagnetic devices.

Undoubtedly, in years to come, we are going to be exposed to more and more of this type of radiation. Time will tell how well we adapt to it. Where strong fields are created – close to pylons, for example – I believe there is grave cause for concern, despite protestations to the contrary by various experts and authorities.

Other Forms of Natural Energy Imbalance

Radioactive energies

Before concluding this chapter, brief mention needs to be made of other forms of natural energy that can cause imbalances within us. I have already written about radiation from radioactive substances. At the moment we are creating some very toxic materials, which will be around for many years to come, in some cases thousands of years. This is fine if the Earth is stable, but we know that radical changes have occurred in the past and we should be conscious that they will certainly happen again in the future. I suspect that most scientists think that future generations will learn how to correct the problems caused by toxic radioactive substances, which will affect long-lived creatures like us more than most other species. So it may be a case of our own chickens coming home to roost.

Radon gas

In areas with high granite levels radon gas, which is a naturally toxic substance that seeps up from the ground, can lead to health problems. These cases are best tested using normal scientific equipment – anything that is part of the physical world, which falls within the electromagnetic spectrum, can be tested in this way. There are devices available to test for radon just as Geiger counters are used to test for radiation. Electromagnetic energies can be tested objectively; subtle energies can only be tested subjectively, through an individual, for example by dowsing.

Chapter 11

Positive Steps to Help the Earth

Grounding our energies

We live on a planet that needs our help. This can take many forms, from simply being mindful of the way in which we dispose of refuse to actively participating in ecological movements.

We each need to consider carefully whether we are being a parasite or a benefactor to our host planet. Ultimately, if humanity remains stuck in the former category the Earth will take steps to correct this imbalance. Indeed, as we shall see in the next chapter, there is reason to believe that we may already have gone beyond the point of no return, at least in the sense of having already invoked some kind of natural backlash, in the form of earthquakes, firestorms, floods, tempests or disease. Yet whatever takes place within the collective we can each take positive steps to bring a sense of balance and harmony into our lives, and to extend that focus to the planet.

Taking responsibility

This is not a task that we should leave to others, for it behoves each of us to make a positive contribution to the home that gives us life and physical experience. The steps in this process are not difficult, although they can be a real challenge for some people. We first need to work on actively linking our energies to those of the Earth, as described in Chapter 1, so that we are resonating in harmony with the planet's vibrational essence. In this we should remember that it is not the Earth which needs to create a harmony with us, but rather the other way round.

In humility, love and respect, we need to discover this new resonance within us. I can assure you that this has to be done consciously – simply thinking that you are in harmony with the Earth is not enough. It is this act of conscious connection which is the most significant single step we can take towards the redemption of humanity on this planet. We need continually to reinforce this link so that the quantum leaps of change that the Earth is undergoing become part of *our* transformation. The process of moving from the Piscean to the Aquarian age[§] will not happen overnight. This transition involves the whole planet, not just human beings, and it is the task of our Planetary Deva to filter and shape these new dynamic forces in a way that is suitable for the evolutionary steps that she/he wishes to undergo.

Balancing the Earth's polarities

We are not the captains of spaceship Earth, that is the task of Gaia/Geb; we are only part of the crew. We have been allowed to develop in the way we have because of the potentially important task that we can fulfil for the planet – the reconciliation of the polarities in the mutant aggressive/subservient gene that permeates all life on this sphere. We are not the only species involved in this

[§]Each age, based upon the precession of the equinoxes, takes about 2,160 years. Since around the time of the birth of Christ it has been the age of Pisces, while the next age will be ruled by the astrological sign of Aquarius.

process, but because of our orientation – i.e. standing vertical – it is easier for us to access the required rebalancing energies from the Solar Lord, the Christ consciousness love that emanates from the Sun, and to help focus these on the matrix of the Earth. Trees are also playing an important role in this transformational process. When one species finds this balance it creates a new resonance that then becomes available to the whole planet.

Balancing our aggressive tendencies

The second important step is for each of us to acknowledge our potential for aggression as well as for subservience (the situation in which many women throughout the world find themselves) and to try to ensure that these energies are balanced within us. In essence we need to acknowledge the existence of both Christ- and Hitler-type energies, and to feel that these energies are fully reconciled within us, for only then will balance be found. This is a crucial and often very painful step. Paradoxically we need to love and embrace our potential for hate and not reject it, for only then can we be truly free of its influence.

There is a powerful moment in the film *Schindler's List* when the camp commandant, having recently shot several Jewish people in the back from his room, turns to Schindler and says, 'To have the ability to shoot someone at will, that is real power.' Schindler replies, 'No, that is not real power. To have the ability to shoot someone at will and then not to shoot them, that is real power.'

It will be a long time yet before real harmony is achieved on this planet. Firm, resolute action is needed to tackle those who wish to cause chaos through the bullet and the bomb. Generally it is necessary first to take away the stick from the man beating the child before he can be helped to relinquish his need to act in this way.

When steps need to be taken collectively to protect our freedoms and the rights of innocent individuals we should proceed with resolution and firmness yet also with equanimity and a sense of forgiveness. We need to listen to the aggressor's point of view. If revenge and hatred lie at the heart of our action then we are only adding to the potential for further hatred and violence.

The fundamental charter of human rights embodies all that we need to aspire to, yet while there is still one person denied these rights because of the intolerance, hatred, fear or domination of another, then there is a battle still to be fought – a battle that must draw on the strengths of both 'hawks' and 'doves'. The rights of individuals, particularly the vulnerable members of society, need to be protected, and when those rights have been enshrined, then it will be time to actively tackle the many issues that led to the feelings of anger and frustration in the first place, and to question what causes individuals to act in the way they sometimes do.

Social imbalances

When a person is physically ill they are treated in hospital or by a doctor and great care is taken to help them on the road to recovery. When a person is socially ill we generally lock them in prison and fail to ask why they have acted in the way they have. We need to question the underlying causes that lead to breaches of the civil code, and then take steps to help the individuals in question face what they have done, guiding them beyond the need for this type of activity.

Globally this is a task for world leaders, whose duty should be to listen to and understand the cries of the disaffected members of their countries. Yet global imbalances are mirrored in microcosm in our own lives. The situation in Palestine between Arabs and Jews, for example, is reflected in everybody's heart at some level or other. Those individuals with whom for whatever reason we have fallen out, or who have fallen out with us, need to be seen as aspects of ourselves. They need to be acknowledged, forgiven and loved, no matter how badly they have treated us, and every possible step needs to be taken to find some form of reconciliation.

The balancing through love and forgiveness of this tortuous polarity of aggression and subservience, of being victim or persecutor, is the only way forward. We are playing out this dynamic for the Earth, and while there is continued hope for its resolution then Gaia/Geb will probably turn a blind eye to our worst excesses. If we get stuck, like the dinosaurs, then the future for humanity will be far from pleasant.

The simple steps in forgiveness are:

1. To forgive others for what they have done to us.

2. To ask for forgiveness (at least inwardly) for any hurt or harm that we have done to others.

3. Finally, and most importantly, to forgive ourselves. This is sometimes the hardest step of all.

Opening the heart

The prerequisite, then, for Aquarian consciousness, is an open heart. The fear-dominated solar plexus orientation of this present age needs to be changed and positive heart-centred steps taken. I am always at a loss to understand why individuals talk about opening the heart chakra before carrying out any healing work and then closing it down again at the end. This seems to me a bit like visiting church once a week and then forgetting about our spirituality for the other six days. What is wrong with always having an open heart? It might be painful at times, we may be hurt, but so what?

Love is the greatest healer, and by continually loving

we purge the dross of our being in the searing heat of its transforming potency. Above all we need to love our own vulnerability, for we can only really love others, consciously or subconsciously, to the extent that we can love and forgive ourselves. The loving of the self allows the magnificence of who and what we are to begin to shine through the obscuring cloaks of our personalities. This also needs to be an ongoing process. The cosmic level of love will only be fully attained when we finally return to our Creator, something to look forward to well after our final incarnation, when we reside on the planes of pure spirit.

It does not matter what symbolism you use for this opening-up process, but seeing your heart chakra as a beautiful open flower is a very easy image to conjure up. We can consciously send out thoughts of love and healing directly from hearts, or imagine that this same energy is being directed through our hands as a focused beam of balancing light. Envelop all that you come into contact with in this gentle panoply and you will be rewarded a thousandfold. In essence we are truly magnificent, amazing beings, who hold all the potential of God within us. As Christ stated, 'The kingdom of heaven is within.' The light of who and what we are needs to shine forth in all its beauty and radiance.

Feeling at home on planet Earth

This leads on to another problem, discussed in Chapter 1 – the fact that many people sense that they do not belong on the Earth or do not feel at home here. They see this world as alien to all that they sense within themselves. There are many reasons for such feelings too complex to go into here. Certainly the way that human beings act and the sort of society that we have created leave much to be desired, but we each need to try to accept that this is our home, at least for this present life.

These feelings of disconnection will not necessarily be resolved overnight, but the steps already given in the Sun/Earth linking exercise in Chapter 1 (see p. 18) will go a long way to helping. We need to feel this link to the Earth through our bodies, and not just in our heads. It is also important to acknowledge the feeling of the Earth not being your home, if that is what you feel, and then try to do everything in your power to be at home here.

The paradox of protection

One of the dynamics that moves through all aspects of creation is that of paradox. It is my firm belief that, in tackling some of the situations discussed in these pages, individuals need to have understood and worked with the concept of protection. And yet I also know that creating a psychic protection, hoping to block out or to ward off something that one deeply fears, tends to invite that situation into one's life, for fear is a powerful magnet. The wife who tries to energetically block out or shield herself from her husband's anger, out of fear, is not really tackling the cause of the problem, which, in part at least, will lie within herself. When you come to put up a protection, ask yourself, 'Am I putting up this protection out of fear?' If the answer is yes, you will need to tackle the root cause of that fear.

As part of our spiritual growth we have to confront and embrace our fears, one by one, for only then can we move on. We should approach psychic protection with the same level of equanimity that we adopt when selecting the clothes we wear to counteract changes in climatic conditions. If it is raining, then we put on a raincoat; if sunny, a hat may be necessary, and so on. There are many different types of protection, some of which we have discussed in these pages. Choose the ones that satisfy you, and do not be afraid to experiment.

The scales of Maat

There are two other techniques worth considering which can provide valuable insights and will help you in dealing with both Earth energy and personal imbalances. The first incorporates the Ancient Egyptian symbolism of the 'scales of Maat'. In the judgement of Osiris the souls of the departed were brought before a tribunal of gods and goddesses to determine whether they were worthy to enter the Osirian heaven.

A key element in this process involved weighing the heart of the deceased on scales against the feather of Truth. Maat was the goddess of divine order, and it was her scales that were used in the weighing ceremony, the verdict being recorded by the god Thoth. Symbolically these scales can be used whenever you want to gain an insight into the truth or balance of any situation.

In carrying out any of these visualised rituals it is best to make the inner connections described in Chapter 1. You then imagine the symbol of the scales in front of you and place the problem on one side of the scales and the feather of Truth on the other and see whether the two balance. If they do not then some difficulty is indicated which can be further assessed. If the answer is not clear, then offer the symbol up to the Sun, asking for clarity in what needs to be done.

You can use this technique to check the effectiveness of any healing work that you have carried out. If the scales balance then you know that everything is all right. If they do not, then more healing work is needed.

The Law of Challenge

The second technique is called the Law of Challenge, and is also helpful in assessing whether a situation is as it first seems. It is principally applied to assessing spirits, but can be used in a wider context if necessary.

Basically all spirits will show their true identity if challenged in the right way. This can be very helpful if you wish to ascertain the source of a channelled message, or if some spirit presents itself purporting to be from the 'light'.

So how do you challenge a spirit?

You will need to imagine a symbol like that of the Celtic or cosmic cross (see Figure 10, p. 189) and then project this image at the spirit, asking inwardly in the name of the Father/Mother God for the spirit to reveal its true identity. If you are clairvoyant you will see a symbol or colour coming back to you. White, gold or blue are all colours associated with teaching spirits. Also, if the cosmic cross remains clear and balanced, then you can rest assured of the validity of the message. If the channeller suddenly breaks off the communication, or the colours or symbols are distorted, then I would be very wary of accepting what has been conveyed.

You can also use this technique on any form of teaching or philosophy. Indeed, you can pick up this book and project the symbol on to it to see what you get.

False guides

Many years ago I received a request to attend a channelling from a being who claimed to be 'the Master'. It was implied that this was the Christ Spirit, and this spirit had some important information for me. There were just three of us in the gathering. The channeller began making some statements that did not ring true, so I issued a mental challenge. Immediately she contradicted what she had said before, and this further alerted me to the fact that something was not right.

The so-called 'Master' wanted me to train as a medium under a particular guide, which I said I was not prepared to do unless I had first consulted my inner teacher, at which point the 'Master' became very angry, saying who was I to question him, and that if I did not do what was requested then my karma would be seriously affected. As I have already stated, no true teaching introduces an element of fear in any way, and this most decidedly was not the Christ Spirit communicating, which both my challenge and its responses had highlighted.

The sad thing about this experience is that I knew that many other individuals had been taken in and no doubt would continue to be so in future for as long as this channeller continued to use her gift to gain domination over others.

Working in groups or individually

Many people reading this book may be unaffiliated to any group or organisation. Tackling some of the more challenging tasks outlined here should only really be taken on within the context of a group. You can always send thoughts of love and balance, with complete safety, no matter what the situation, so the individual can achieve a tremendous amount on their own.

However, if you can find a few friends to link up with then the potential for more specific healing is increased considerably. The challenge for any group is finding harmony, and this requires a willingness to listen and to appreciate the contribution that others make.

Black sheep

In my experience of groups there is often one individual who elects or is elected to express the shadow aspects of the team. This can be a source of enormous irritation, because that individual will often be seen as the cause of disharmony. And yet if steps are taken to remove that person then the group will often collapse for all sorts of other reasons. So I would strongly encourage all those who want to work within a group structure to be very wary of expelling a member just because they are difficult. The more we see people as reflections of ourselves, the more we can inwardly look at what is going on and then deal with it in a positive way. You will also have to deal with many different egos and this too can be a severe challenge.

Group work is not easy, and will inevitably awaken all sorts of interpersonal problems. It is rather like bright sunlight shining through a window in the spring. What seemed clean one day can reveal itself to be very dirty the next. In invoking the light you inevitably highlight your shadow, which has to be acknowledged and faced in order to find balance. As we move forward into the Aquarian age, and these dynamics become more balanced within us, then the shadow aspects will be held by all individuals within a group, and not just by one person, so group work will become easier.

Group potential

If – and it is a big if – you can find group harmony, then the potential for some very powerful healing work becomes possible. I would urge you to commit to work together for a given period, and also to keep the numbers low. Better three people working in harmony than 50 whose energies are all over the place. There is a role for large groups in sending out healing energies together, but the power generated by three people fusing their energy into a laser beam can potentially accomplish much more than 1,000 people trying to hold up candles on a windy night.

Power centres

To access the full depth of energy within a landscape power centre you will need to have reached a certain level of inner balance and development. The power afforded by this connection can give a considerable boost to the effectiveness of any healing or inner development work. My strong recommendation would be to give yourself plenty of time to seek out those places that can afford you spiritual uplift and insight. When you reach a level at which you can begin to communicate with the guardian of the centre, then you may be afforded the opportunity of drawing on some of that energy for your healing work, provided your intentions are selfless. If you try to use the energy for power or gain then it will simply be blocked or, worse, you may suffer a backlash.

Dangers

There are some very powerful energies within the cosmos. Your chances of physical survival if a nuclear explosion took place next to you would be minimal. The power of subtle energies is equally impressive. Their incorrect use has destroyed past civilisations and can potentially do so again, yet on the other hand they can be used for great healing and rebalancing.

It is important to tread carefully, ensuring that on each step of the journey your feet are planted firmly on the earth before you take the next step. Above all, if you approach this exploration with an open, loving heart you will receive the divine guidance that will cherish and nurture your every move. There will, of course, be times when you will stumble, but this is all part of the learning process.

Right or wrong?

One of the most inhibiting polarity dynamics is trying to be 'right' or to do the 'right' thing. I am not talking here about what is morally right or wrong but about the direction of a person's life, whether to go one way or another. As soon as you move to one extreme of the polarity you immediately invite the other extreme into your psyche, and become embroiled in the pendulum swing of being pulled between right and wrong. All life is experience, and some experiences are more challenging than others; that is all. Do what your heart dictates, without worrying about whether it is right or wrong, and your journey through life will be full of richness.

At a somatic level at least we are part of the Earth. We only have to look around our planet to see its amazing beauty as well as the desecration inflicted on our world. There is nothing wrong with technology – it provides new experiences for the many different spheres of consciousness on this planet. What we need to strive for is a technology that is Earth-friendly rather than one that potentially pollutes and destroys the habitats and environments of the majority of the Earth's denizens.

At the moment it is not easy to see the correlation between good husbandry and economic benefit. Soon there will be no doubt in the minds of big-business executives and world leaders that there is a price to be paid when the ecological factor is not taken into account. Extremes of weather are but a foretaste of what may come.

At the moment insurance companies pick up the financial bill for the abuse of the environment through pollution when nature responds with flood, hurricane or fire. This is a short-sighted approach, for it is much better to tackle the root cause of the problem and not pollute in the first place.

There is certainly nothing wrong with cars and similar forms of transport, but why do they need to be driven by oil-derived fuels that have environmental consequences? Collectively we need to seek forms of fuel that are harmonious to the Earth, which do not upset the balance of the planet or cause problems to the elemental realms.

Physical pollution is but one aspect, for mental pollution, through anger and hatred, is just as toxic, and perhaps even more insidiously pervasive, for its effects are not so apparent.

Awakening to our spiritual and physical heritage

There is still much to be done before we take our rightful place on Earth in full harmony with the spiritual and physical realms around us. By taking small steps in our lives, by trying to be more conscious of the subtle realms of the Earth, we can make a valuable and positive contribution to our planet.

Chapter 12
The Psyche of the Earth

We have journeyed through a number of different aspects of Earth healing and working with Earth energies. It would be remiss in a book such as this if we did not allow the Earth her/himself a voice in these proceedings. But before opening up a dialogue with what is generally known as Gaia, we should first set out our stall and briefly consider the Earth's history and evolution.

The birth of the Earth

Scientists tell us that the Earth was born about 4,600 million years ago as a fiery mass of energy spewed out from the Sun. As the Earth cooled, land masses and oceans began to appear, with the oldest known rocks dating to around 3,800 million years. It took another 300 million years for the first sea-based micro-organisms to appear, and from these small beginnings more complex life forms started to develop. The period of time from the birth of the Earth up to 600 million years ago is called the Precambrian epoch, and saw the first emergence of plants, sea creatures and a more diverse eco-system that, in turn, led to the formation of our present atmospheric balance.

Around 200 million years ago the entire land mass of

the planet was focused on one super-continent called Pangaea (from the Greek word meaning 'all earth'). Shortly after this Pangaea split into two, a northern half called Laurasia, which included North America, Greenland, Europe and Asia, and a southern portion called Gondwanaland, which included Africa, South America, Antarctica, Australasia and Indonesia.

The first dinosaurs emerged during this epoch, and over the next 170 million years the continents slowly assumed the shapes we know today. As most people are aware, the dinosaurs died out around 65 million years ago following a comet impact in the Gulf of Mexico, which had devastating consequences for the whole Earth.

Human beings are most closely related genetically to chimpanzees, and our earliest common ancestor probably lived around 4 million years ago. It was not until about 150,000 years ago that a genetic mutation occurred somewhere in southern Africa which led to the birth of modern man. In terms of the Earth's history we, as a species, are a newcomer to this planet.

Structure of the planet

Planet Earth has an equatorial circumference of 24,903 miles (40,077 kilometres) with an average radius of 3,958 miles (6,370 kilometres). There is a slight flattening at the poles, which means that we are not quite a perfect sphere.

The outer skin of the planet is called the crust, and has a depth of approximately 33 kilometres. The deepest mine in the world is the Western Deep Levels mine in South Africa, which penetrates 3,581 metres below ground level. Everything below this point has been mapped by detecting sound waves from earthquakes in different regions of the planet. From this we know that the Earth has a solid inner core composed of iron and helium surrounded by a liquid fiery outer core. The mantle is made up of semi-molten rocks. The Earth turns on its axis every 24 hours and circles the Sun in a little over 365 days.

Our Moon is somewhat unusual, being very much larger than would be expected in the normal circumstances of planetary development. This has led some astronomers to suggest that the Earth and Moon should be viewed as a binary planetary system. Scientists now believe that the Moon was originally part of the Earth and was split off at a very early stage of the planet's history when a large comet crashed into the Earth.

Comet impacts

Recent discoveries about the frequency of comet impacts have suggested that these are more common than at first thought, and that even human history has been shaped by sudden cataclysmic events bringing severe changes in climate to different regions of the globe.

From around 100,000 years ago the Earth was in the grip of an ice age, which did not abate until about 13,000 BC. At the moment we are in what is termed the sub-boreal epoch, which started around 3200 BC with a slight cooling in the climatic conditions of the Earth. However, the recent use of fossil fuels has started to reverse this trend, and at the moment scientists are trying to evaluate the effects of global warming, which is likely to continue well into the first part of this new millennium.

Throughout the history of the planet many species have evolved and then become extinct. The pressures of human expansion have accelerated this process for many of the present species on the planet; indeed, this has led one scientist to suggest that we are in a period of mass extinction that rivals that which caused the destruction of the dinosaurs. However, we should not lose sight of the fact that this has happened before in the history of the Earth, and would appear to be part of a natural process.

The planet of music and healing

The Earth is part of the solar system, which contains at least nine planets – Mercury, Venus, Earth, Mars, Jupiter, Saturn, Uranus, Neptune and Pluto – and a host of smaller objects, including the asteroids and planetoid bodies like Chiron.

There are some indications that there is another planetary body beyond that of Pluto, and esoteric sources claim the existence of a small planet called Vulcan, close to the Sun, within the orbit of Mercury. However, this has not been validated by astronomers at the present time.

Each planet in the solar system is assigned a particular quality in astrological terms. Mercury, for example, is the planet of communication, while Venus is the planet of love. Earth is the planet of music and healing. This interpretation could be expanded to suggest that its energies are suitable for helping spirits find inner balance, as well as providing a playground of sonic resonances to be explored. Nature provides a myriad of different sounds through birds, insects and aquatic life, so it is not just human beings who are venturing into and exploring the world of music.

The Gaia hypothesis

The concept of Gaia came to the fore with the publication of Jim Lovelock's ground-breaking book on the Gaia hypothesis, in which he looked for the conditions that indicated the existence of life on a planet. His initial remit was to assess whether life existed on Mars, but in order to make such an evaluation he needed to understand the process here on Earth. He realised that conditions on Earth, which make life as we know it possible, were maintained in a dynamic state, unlike those of other planets.

The Gaia hypothesis proposes that our planet functions as a single organism that maintains conditions necessary for its survival. In order to do this various systems work together to maintain conditions suitable for life in its many diverse forms. Lovelock came to the startling conclusion that the different self-regulating mechanisms seemed to imply a form of global consciousness because life was self-sustaining.

For example, the necessary balance of atmospheric gases needed to support life, such as oxygen, was maintained through a series of checks and balances that implied conscious intent. The present level of oxygen in our atmosphere (21 per cent) is ideal. If it were to increase by only a few percentage points the atmosphere would combust, burning everything to a cinder. If it dropped below 18 per cent, life as we know it would cease to exist. Balance is maintained because various organisms on this planet work together to make sure that oxygen levels are kept within this narrow band.

Lovelock adopted the name Gaia from Greek mythology, although he never went so far as to suggest that this global consciousness was focused in a specific being or entity. However, many New Age groups seized upon Lovelock's idea and took it to imply the existence of a being called Gaia.

Throughout history, and through different cultures, the Earth spirit has been ascribed many different names. As has been stated, to the Ancient Egyptians the Earth was Geb, while the sky was the great goddess Nut. In Sumerian mythology the Earth was also male, known as Enki (the 'Lord Earth'), a god of wisdom. However, in most mythologies the Earth is represented by a female deity – the Mother Earth concept.

The Gaia Dialogues

In a remarkable book by Murry Hope entitled *The Gaia Dialogues*, the author describes her communications with the spirit of Gaia, and what she has to say about her evolution and the impact of human beings on her sphere. The book makes uncomfortable reading because, not surprisingly, Gaia does not appreciate the proliferation of human activity and indicates that she will soon take action to cull a large proportion of the population, through a global cataclysm, by effecting a change in the axis of the Earth, which at the moment is set at about 22.5 degrees to the ecliptic.

There is scientific evidence that axis tilt changes have happened before. Indeed, these may be the explanation for some of the long-term changes in climatic conditions, although generally these have not been seen as being caused by cataclysmic events, as implied by Murry Hope's communications, but rather as gradual modification over several thousand years.

Danuih

Hope also suggests that Gaia prefers to be called Danuih, which, we are told, correlates more accurately with her sonic vibrations. In these dialogues Danuih affirms that the other part of her polarity, the yang half, will be manifesting its presence in the near future – in other words, the Earth represents a balance of polarities. This accords well with my own connections with the Earth, as has been indicated throughout this book. I do think it is very important, for many different reasons, that we see the Earth as representing both polarities, the Gaia/Geb blend, which allows us to experience a balance in the way we relate to the Earth at a spiritual level.

It is seven years since Hope wrote her book, so has the situation changed? Are we still going to experience a global cataclysm as Gaia communicated to her? I believe it is within everyone's capabilities to tune into the Earth to arrive at their own assessment, so what is presented here should be judged by what you yourself believe to be true. Using the image of the being that first appeared to me more than 27 years ago, I have established my own level of communication with the Earth spirit, and the following is what has been relayed to me.

Gaia/Geb speaks

I appreciate this opportunity to convey a sense of my beingness to those who read these pages. It is necessary for you to realise that my level of awareness and consciousness is so very different from your own. Like you I have an understanding of, and a connection to, my physical body, the Earth, yet I am not Earth centred in my exploration into the nature of reality.

My time, if that is the right word, is taken up by communications with other spiritual essences, which are of a similar evolution to myself, and in this my thoughts reach out to the most distant galaxies that your astronomers can detect, for communication takes place on many different levels within the cosmos and in dimensions that you have not as yet even begun to imagine.

My physical body is home to vast numbers of spirits, from the fiery depths of my innermost parts to the vast oceans and atmosphere that make up my globe, in the same way that within you there are many spirit forms and microscopic life essences.

Unlike you I can be conscious of and connect to the smallest life essence on my sphere. But very rarely do I take steps to change the dynamic of what is happening unless it becomes a necessary part of my evolutionary process. Like you I have a life plan and a destiny to fulfil, which is not conditioned but reflects the consensus of the patterning established by our Solar Lord. In other words all planets within this system have elected to fulfil certain tasks as a way of providing a full range of spiritual experience.

Physical life, as you will discover, does exist on other spheres within this solar system although nothing like to the same extent that is witnessed here. My sphere does provide a unique range of experiences for sentient life to a level not generally found within this galaxy. Most life essences on other spheres experience only to a level of density that you have described as etheric.

As I know you are also aware, I have, in recent times, had a difficult relationship with my companion, which you call Moon, which has held the matrix of a devic spirit that has caused me much discomfort. You have ascribed the name Lucifer to this essence, although I would use a different name.

This essence has exaggerated the seed imbalance that you have described already in your book. The resolution of that dynamic, which you have called aggression, with that of extreme subservience has been something that I elected to take on for the Solar Lord. This has meant that many souls visiting my sphere have come specifically to experience these extremes and through that experience to find some form of resolution, some form of balance.

The control that Lucifer imposed on my sphere has now been lessened, thanks to the help of that essence you know as Mikkael. With his help I have been able to stabilise the force exerted by the Moon and this will, in itself, see a lessening of the extremes of violence that my body has witnessed through many different forms of life, not just human beings.

I must confess that there has always been a reluctance within me to accept the invasion of your species into my domain, for I knew that it would bring with it much pain and suffering. But I was persuaded by our Solar Lord that this would be for the best in the long term, and it is only now that I can begin to glimpse the import of what was then suggested.

Of course, there have been those of your species that have acknowledged and revered me but these, comparatively, have been very few, and even then they have been open to committing terrible atrocities against their fellow human beings. In this sense my connecting with all those species on this sphere is primarily that of witness and observer, only taking steps to interfere when absolutely necessary, for I acknowledge and respect the free-will gift that has been bestowed on all life essences by the Creator.

However, you can be very sure that I will not allow this world, my sphere, to be needlessly destroyed by your aggressive tendencies. It is the cosmic right of all spirits to take whatever steps are necessary to defend their integrity, their ability to experience. Should there be a danger of you unleashing forces that could destroy my body, and it is possible, then very powerful counter-measures would be brought to bear to prevent this happening.

As part of my evolution I also go through initiatory jumps, which allow me to take on and experience new ranges of vibratory energy. There will be changes taking place within the body of the solar system which will affect the way that I relate to my brother and sister planets and to the Sun. These will have an effect on my physical structure and orbit, which in turn will affect all the physical land masses of my sphere.

The timing of these changes is not fixed but is dependent upon many events synchronising themselves, so I cannot relay to you precisely when this will take place in terms of your Earth years, but it will happen, of that you can be sure. How you relate to these changes will be dependent upon the level of understanding and cooperation that you have reached. Some essences will certainly choose to leave incarnation at this time but others will have the option of staying or leaving dependent upon what they have been able to integrate within themselves. The more that you as a species can find a balance within yourselves, and learn to work in harmony with the other life essences of my world, the less will be the impact of my step-up of energy frequency upon you. So the choice is yours, not mine.

Nature is often seen as amoral, in that the forces of nature on this planet do not take account of the impact they have upon other physical life essences. I acknowledge your fear of death, but this is something considered strange within the devic realms, of which I am a part, which sees all life as but transition from one state to another.

When the Solar Lord came to this planet through the vehicle of the man that you call Jesus Christ, he brought instruction to all the beings of my sphere about the need to respect life. For our part we have been trying to assimilate this teaching, and where necessary to curtail the potential for acting precipitously when confronted by the worst excesses which human beings have perpetrated upon my sphere.

This has meant that the elemental and devic forces have for the most part shown considerable restraint over the past 2,000 years, which would not have happened but for the intervention of the Solar Lord. Those who are able to find harmony with these teachings and with the new impulses of my sphere will know within themselves where they will need to be, to be safe when the more dramatic events unfold in the future. Those that cannot make the necessary shift in consciousness, and this applies to all species, will leave incarnation and in some cases whole species will cease to exist. The potential truly is for the lion to lie down with the lamb.

My love and care are there for every life essence on my sphere. Open your hearts to what is offered here and your lives will be enriched in ways beyond your wildest dreams. This is the promise of the Solar Lord, and I bow to the wisdom of that message.

I cannot do more than express my own deep gratitude to the Earth and all those spiritual beings who have helped me on my journey through life. This planet is without doubt an amazing place to experience.

Healing ourselves, healing our planet

This book has been a journey into the ways in which we can each influence and help the Earth. In return we cannot help but be helped ourselves to find a new level of balance and awareness, for it is always a two-way process. As you give out, so you will receive. There is an enormous amount to be done to clear some of the toxic mental energies that our species has liberally scattered across the globe. By learning to connect to and communicate with the deva and elemental kingdoms we open up a treasure chest of amazing experience. We can only do this when we open our hearts, and by opening our hearts to these other realms we potentially open our hearts to everyone and everything; to life itself. This is a wonderful gift.

With an open heart it is much easier to forgive and let go, not only of our own negative karmic attachments but also of all those things that stop us fully expressing ourselves as the magnificent beings that we truly are, making our daily life a joy to experience.

Appendix

The eighth chakra

In Chapter 3 I mentioned an eighth chakra. Those used to working with only seven chakras may have wondered why I introduced an eighth, so the more detailed explanation given here is certainly appropriate.

The concept of the chakras stems from ancient yogic traditions which maintain that there are spiritual energy centres focused in specific places across the front of the body. The Sanskrit word chakra literally means *wheel*, and suggests the spiralling, pulsating, vibrational quality of these energy points. Different symbols, sounds and god names were assigned to each of the chakras, but interestingly enough the symbolic connection of the seven colours of the spectrum is a relatively modern Western addition, being introduced in the 1920s by Charles Leadbeater, one of the leaders of the Theosophical movement. It never formed part of the original tradition.

Most people are aware of the placement of these chakras, which are normally given Western names rather than their Sanskrit originals. The Sahasrara chakra is the crown on the top of the head, the Ajna chakra is known as the brow, while the throat is the Visuddha. The heart chakra symbolised by two interlocking and inverted triangles, like the Star of David, is called the Anahata, and the Manipura chakra is located at the solar plexus. The lower abdomen or sacral is the position for the Svadhisthana chakra, while the chakra at the base of the spine is known as the Muludhara.

A study of Hindu texts makes it clear that they too suggested many additional minor chakric points, and there were also differences in Tantric Buddhist traditions, which adopted the chakric concepts. But the main focus of seven chakras has endured for a very long time. So why do I suggest a change?

Part of my karmic task through more than 30 years' study and exploration into metaphysical subjects has been to discover the underlying essence within all spiritual traditions. We live in amazing times on this planet, for never before in the history of the world have so many traditions been so readily accessible to us.

We can now explore Chinese, Tibetan, Ancient Egyptian, Celtic, cabbalistic, shamanistic and many more traditions with considerable ease. This is a unique gift, allowing people to walk again along those spiritual paths that their soul has experienced before in its karmic journey through different incarnations. The underlying principles in all these traditions must, like the laws of physics, be consistent. God would not have created a different set of principles for each tradition. They must all be recognising the same underlying matrix and then be translating it into a form that makes sense for them.

Throughout my life I have been deeply interested in patterns – the patterns that can be found in the landscape, the patterns that weave through our lives, and the patterns that can be found by comparing different spiritual traditions. Spiritual truths are consistent through all traditions and mythologies, so the intrinsic patterns that we find replicated in one tradition must be and are, in whole or in part, reflected in another.

Eight primary principles

Through many years of research I have come to recognise that there are eight distinct primary spiritual principles, which revolve around a central core of light generally symbolised by the Sun. This is most apparent in the eight trigrams of the I Ching, which form the basis of the eight directions in feng shui. The Scandinavian and Germanic runes are divided into three Aettir of eight runes each, and there are eight main festivals in Celtic mythology.

Many other associations can also be found through all the major mythologies, too numerous to mention here. Because of this eightfold patterning I have, for a long time, felt that collectively humanity needs to be working with eight main chakras and not seven – a proposal that has been powerfully endorsed by my spiritual teachers on the inner planes.

Others, too, have recognised this need, but in most cases any additions to the chakric system are placed in the upper part of the body or even above the head. A significant aspect of my incarnation has been the recognition that it is vital to our well-being to fully ground ourselves within the physical body, and more important still to align our energies with those of the pulse of the Earth.

Our planet is going through a major transformational shift, with new frequencies becoming available to us all the time; we need to be continually updating our connection with these new vibrant Earth energies to keep pace with the changing dynamic of our planet.

The root chakra

The connection to the ground is through our feet. They are crucial to this process, for it is through our feet that we can connect with the vibrational energies of the Earth. For many years now I have worked with the feet as the eighth chakra, which I feel should be appropriately named the root chakra. The energy of this chakra not only connects us with the planet, but also with our roots or origins. Its energy helps us access past lives and karmic patterns, as well as the genetic blueprint that we receive from our parents, and above all it helps root us firmly in the vibrational essence of the Earth

The feet are significant in two other ways. It was the feet of His disciples which Jesus washed. In this act he was drawing attention to the importance of the feet and also washing away past karmic imbalances. We too can do the same for ourselves by washing our own feet. Second, the feet are used as a primary focus of treatment in reflexology. This would only be possible if the feet themselves carried a chakric impulse, with a special quality that allows it to be used in helping to rebalance the other systems of the body.

The archetype or god form that I associate with this chakra is the Greek god Hermes or his Roman equivalent Mercury, who wears winged sandals and carries in his hand the caduceus staff, the symbol of healing, with its entwining snakes and wings at the top.

Colours and the chakras

We have already discussed how we can introduce an eighth colour for the root chakra (see p. 68). However, I do not really like the usual ordered association of colours with the chakras for, in my experience, they do not work in reality.

For example, on many occasions within groups I have run over the years I have asked individuals to tune into the quality of love and then to determine the colour that they inwardly felt reflected this love. I have then asked them to suggest where in their body they felt the focus of their love to be. In the vast majority of cases the heart was seen as the focus of love energy.

In terms of colours blue, pink and deep red are the most commonly ascribed; very rarely green, the traditional colour associated with the heart chakra. I would prefer to mix up the traditional chakra colours, as shown below. The list is not meant to be definitive but to act as a spur to further thought.

1. Crown – magenta (although some people prefer white or gold)
2. Brow – violet
3. Throat – yellow
4. Heart – blue
5. Solar plexus – orange
6. Sacral – turquoise
7. Base – red
8. Root – green

By locating the eighth chakra on the soles of the feet we create a balance with the crown chakra and a point of contact with the Earth in a way not considered before. To fulfil our collective karmic task we have to go through this process of Earth linking, of Earth harmonisation. The root chakra allows this to happen.

Minor planetary chakric areas

I have already given the minor planetary chakric areas for Europe (see pp. 69–70). Here are my suggestions for the other continents of the Earth. It should be appreciated that these are broad regions and not focused on specific places.

	Africa	Asia	Australasia
Crown	Atlas Mountains	Tibet, Nepal	Central Australia
Brow	Egypt & Nubia	India	New Zealand
Throat	Ethiopia	Japan	SE Australia
Heart	Lake Victoria, Tanzania	Gobi Desert	New Guinea
Solar plexus	Sahara & West Africa	Siberia	Queensland
Sacral	Congo Basin	China	Indonesia, Borneo
Base	Namibia, Kalahari	Burma, Thailand	Western Australia
Root	Table Mountain, South Africa	Afghanistan, Iran	Tasmania

	North America/Canada	South America	Arctic
Crown	Lake Superior area	Lake Titicaca area	Lapland
Brow	California	Ecuador	Hudson Bay
Throat	New York, Washington	Peru	Iceland
Heart	Four corner states of SW	Amazonia/Brazil	Central Siberia
Solar plexus	Lake Erie	Argentina	Alaska
Sacral	Mississippi, Florida area	Colombia	Greenland
Base	Mexico	Patagonia	NE Siberia
Root	Caribbean	Tierra del Fuego	North Siberia

Sacred sites around the world

The following is a list of some of the sacred sites around the world that can be used for healing and balance.

1. Britain:

England:	Arbor Low stone circle, Derbys.; Glastonbury Tor, Somerset; Stonehenge, Wilts.; Avebury, Wilts.; Worcester Beacon, Malvern Hills, Worcs.; Canterbury Cathedral, Kent; Castlerigg stone circle, Cumberland; Lindisfarne Monastery, Northumberland; Roughtor, Bodmin Moor, Cornwall; St Michael's Mount, Cornwall
Wales:	Cader Idris, Gwynedd; St David's, Pembrokeshire
Scotland:	Arthur's Seat, Edinburgh; Ring of Brodgar stone circle, Orkneys; Callanish, Western Isles; Iona Cathedral, Hebrides
Ireland:	Rock of Cashel, Tipperary; Glendalough Monastery, Wicklow; Innishfallen Monastery, Kerry; Newgrange burial mound, Meath; Tara, seat of high kings of Ireland, Meath; Croagh Patrick mountain, Co Mayo

2. Europe:

Austria:	Hallstatt, ancient burial grounds
Bulgaria:	Stone Forest, Lake Varna
Crete:	Knossos
Cyprus:	Aphrodite's Rock
Denmark:	Trundholm ritual site
Finland:	Helsinki Cathedral, Helsinki; Saana Mountain, Lapland

France:	Chartres Cathedral, Eure-et-Loir; Cluny Monastery, Burgundy; Le Grand Menhir, Carnac; Le Mont-Saint-Michel, Normandy; Lourdes holy well, Haute Pyrénées
Germany:	Externsteine Rocks, North Germany; Golloring, near Mainz; Manching Celtic site; Stockach burial site, Tübingen
Greece:	Mt Athos; Temple of Apollo, Delphi; Acropolis, Athens; Mycenae, Peloponnese
Italy:	Temple of Minerva, Assisi, Umbria; Florence Cathedral; St Peter's, Rome
Malta:	Ggantija, Gozo; Tarxian
Netherlands:	Papeloze Kerk, Sleen; Utrecht Cathedral
Norway:	Nordkapp, Finnmark; Nidarus Cathedral, Trondheim
Poland:	Church of Virgin Mary, Krakow
Portugal:	Almendras stone circle, Guadalupe
Russia:	Ipatevsky Monastery, Kostroma; Khamar Daban Monastery, Siberia; Kizhi Island, Kareliya; St Sergius Monastery of the Trinity, Zagorsk
Spain:	Altamira, Santander; Los Millares, megalithic site, Santa Fé de Mondújar; Santiago de Compostela Cathedral
Sweden:	Gamla burial mound, Uppsala; Gotland, Viking graves
Turkey:	Mt Ararat, sacred mountain; Catal Huyuk, ancient site, southern Anatolia; Ephesus, temple site; Santa Sophia, Istanbul

3. Asia:

Borneo:	Borobudur, Buddhist temple site
Burma:	Pagan, temple site
China:	Caves of the Thousand Buddhas; Temple of Heaven, Beijing; Shi Huangdi, X'ian; Emeishan
India:	Varanasi (Benares); Bodh Gaya; Golden Temple of Amritsar
Israel:	Dome of the Rock, Jerusalem
Japan:	Mt Fuji; Sumiyoshi, Osaka; The Grand Shrine at Ise; Nara, Horyuji
Saudi Arabia:	Mecca, sacred Islamist site; Medina, sacred Islamist site
Thailand:	Wat Phra Keo, Temple of the Emerald Buddha, Bangkok
Tibet:	Mt Kailas; Jokhang temple, Lhasa
Ukraine:	Caves Monastery, Kiev
Uzbekistan:	Samarkand

4. North America:

Alaska:	Denali (Mt McKinley)
Arizona:	Cathedral Rock, Sedona; Wupatki, Hopi reservation; San Francisco Peaks, sacred mountain
California:	Mount Shasta, sacred mountain
Connecticut:	Sleeping Giant Mountain
Georgia:	Stone Mountain, Atlanta; Etowah Mounds, burial mounds
Hawaii:	Kilauea volcano
Illinois:	Cahokia mounds, burial mounds
Indiana:	Great Circle Mound, ritual site
New Mexico:	Chaco Canyon, ritual site; Mt Taylor, sacred mountain
New York:	Niagara Falls
Ohio:	Serpent Mounds, ritual site
Washington:	Tahoma (Mt Ranier)

Wyoming: Big Horn Medicine Wheel

5. Central America:

Mexico: Teotihuacan; Chichen Itza, Yucatan
Guatemala: Tikal

6. South America:

Bolivia: Lake Titicaca, sacred lake;
               Tiahuanaco, ancient site
Peru: Cuzco, Inca city; Machu Picchu, Inca
               city

7. Australasia:

Australia: Uluru or Ayers Rock; The Olgas
New Zealand: Mt Tongariro, sacred mountain

8. Africa:

Egypt: Great Pyramid, Giza; St Catherine's
               Mountain, Sinai; Hatshepsut temple,
               Luxor; Hathor's temple, Denderah
Gambia: Wassu stone circle
Kenya: Mt Kenya, sacred mountain
Morocco: Atlas Mountains
South Africa: Table Mountain
Zimbabwe: Great Zimbabwe, ancient site

For details of courses and workshops in 'Working with Earth Energies', and for CD on guided images, please contact David Furlong: tel: +44 (0)1684 569105 or 0777 978 9047; e-mail atlanta@dial.pipex.com; www.atlanta-association.com.

Mythology comparison chart

Primary qualities	Greek pantheon	Egyptian *Tarot*	Teutonic/ *Arthurian*	Chinese *I Ching*	Symbols	Colours	Chakras	Animals	Other attributes
Initiation 1	Zeus Hestia	Osiris *Hierophant*	Thor (Donar) *Galahad*	Ch'ien *Father*	Sun disk Crown (golden)	MAGENTA Gold	Crown	lion, tiger, buffalo, horse	Philosophy, direction, universal brotherhood, unity, leadership
Transformation 2	Hera Ares	Seth *Devil*	Loki *Morgan Le Fay*	K'an *Middle son*	Cube Square Crescent	RED Dark green (Black)	Base	pig, bat, rat, fox, hare, Pegasus	Danger, courage, hardship, cleansing, baptism, force, transformation
Exploration 3	Hades Demeter	Anubis *Fool*	Heimdall *Gawaine*	Ken *Youngest son*	Column Pillar	ORANGE Dark blue Black	Solar plexus	dog, white owl, coyote, raven	Research, faith, inner perception, discovery, stillness, joking, clowning
Formation 4	Apollo Artemis	Horus *Emperor*	Tyr (Tiw) *Launcelot*	Li *Middle daughter*	Eye Pentangle 5-pointed star Lyre	YELLOW	Throat	falcon, eagle, swan	Clarity, beauty expressed through arts, crafts and business, acting, prophecy, divination

Communication 5	Hermes —	Thoth *Magician*	Odin (Wodan) *Merlin*	Chen *Eldest son*	Triangle Pyramid Feather Caduceus	GREEN Lilac	Feet	ibis, crow, monkey, snake	Growth, balance, evolution, karma, truth, justice, law, arousal, healing
Organisation 6	Aphrodite Hephaestus	Isis *High Priestess*	Freyja *Guinevere*	K'un *Mother*	Ankh Star of David 6-pointed star Blue cloak	BLUE Turquoise	Heart	dove, deer, unicorn	Love, compassion, selflessness, gentleness, care, forgiveness
Contemplation 7	Poseidon Persephone	Nepthys *Hermit*	Frigg *Lady of the Lake*	Sun *Eldest daughter*	Circle Chalice Lotus Pink Rose	INDIGO Pink Light green	Sacral	fish, dolphin	Reflection, peace, revelation, psychic receptivity, meditation, relaxation
Innovation 8	Athene —	Hathor *Empress*	Balder *Arthur*	Tui *Youngest daughter*	Cross in circle Flaming sword White rose	VIOLET White Electric blue	Brow	lioness, cow, cat, bear, elephant	Joy, insight, protection, spiritual nourishment, intuition, music

Index